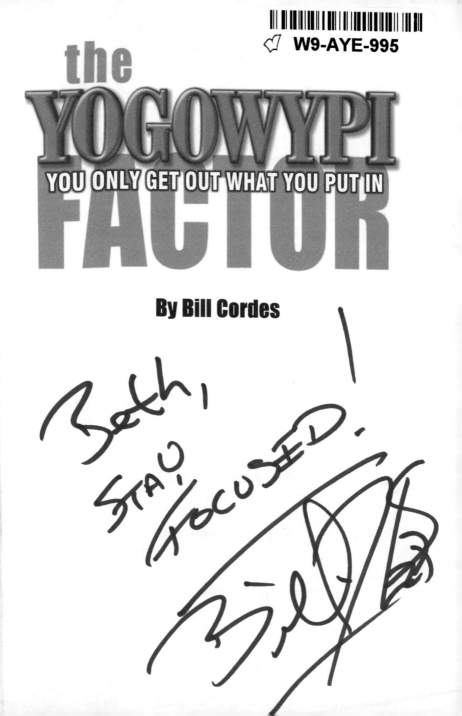

the YOGOWYPI
YOU ONLY GET OUT WHAT YOU PUT IN
FACTOR

By Bill Cordes

Beth,
STAY FOCUSED.

Bill

the YOGOWYPI
YOU ONLY GET OUT WHAT YOU PUT IN
FACTOR

The author is grateful for permission to include this
previously copyrighted material:
"And They Were Taught the Laws of Life..." from
Ano Ano: The Seed by Kristin Zambucka

Cover design by Butch M Graphic Art

ISBN: 09728345-3-2

CONTENTS

1. YOGOWYPI? YOGOWYPI!   3

YOGOWYPI:
2. The Message Behind the Simple Truth   13

3. Y = You Choose Your Approach   23

4. O = O-Zone   37

5. G = Great Efforts Yield Great Rewards   51

6. O = O2 Be Responsible   65

7. W = Wisdom of Mission   85

Y = Y2 Learn:
8. Six Helpful Learning Tools   105

Y = Y2 Learn:
9. Six Character Traits of Successful Students   119

10. P = People Are People-People by Design   145

11. P = People-People Understand Communication 159

12. Integration   177

Notes   184

About the Author   185

Dedication

To the family of the original "YOGOWYPI Man" - Dr. Jim Costigan. He was much more than a teacher to all of us and it is in his memory that I dedicate this book. Thanks for sharing a wonderful man with the world. It was all the people around him that made him great, and I have been blessed because you allowed him to be with us.

To Delorese for teaching me to be Kupa'a, and for your courage and willingness to honor the teens of Hawai'i and the world. Your wisdom is the tapestry of this book.

To every student who has struggled as I have. May your struggles lead you to a life of joy, love and purpose.

To my Dad for instilling in me the values of honesty, character and the importance of a hard days work. I work harder because you taught me that if it was worth doing, it was worth doing right.

To my Mom for giving me the quiet confidence to walk in the direction of my dreams. For standing firm in the face of adversity and for your lifes' demonstration of commitment to the ones you love.

Mostly, this book is dedicated to my loving wife Karla and to my children Josha, Shannon, and Easton. Thanks for the inspiration.

Acknowledgments

Thank you Craig Hillier for your constant encouragement and support. I know you were the source that convinced me to write this book. Thank you for pushing me. You are a wonderful friend, and I am richer because I have known you.

Raymond Bechard...thanks for being a great friend, mentor and a demonstration of how a man should live a life. Your calm presence, unshakable character and desire to bring out the best in others are a powerful force of inspiration.

Barry Fisher...thanks for standing with me when I didn't have the courage to stand alone.

Paul Hedlund...thank you for your many words of wisdom, but mostly thank-you for walking the walk of "True North".

A special thank you to Joleen Roehlkepartan for working so dilegently and for your ability to see what I could never see. You have a wonderful gift with words.

Thank you Karla, for holding it all together when I am out in the world. You are my hero, and I am blessed to have such a wonderful wife. Thank you Josha, Shannon and Easton for giving up so much of our time to make this project possible. Thank you for making my life joy-filled so that I can support others in finding their joy!

How to use "The YOGOWYPI Factor"

The principles applied in this book are timeless and ageless, and can bring value to anyone who is willing to put forth the effort to make positive changes. However, this book was specifically designed for young adults who are amidst transition. If you are in your first year of college, vocational school or just now leaving high school you should be excited about your journey because you are designing your life and you never really know what is around the next corner. Since you are in a time of challenge and design I have written the perfect book for you to assist you in your transition. At the end of each chapter you will discover questions and exercises designed to make you think about where you are and where you are going. Do the exercises. If you are using this book as a text get involved in the class discussions and argue both sides of the issue. This book should be used to help you gain clarity and to support you in making positive life choices.

If your days of young adulthood are far behind you and for whatever reason you picked up this book just know that there is something in here for you as well. These are concepts that I am still wrestling with and working to understand. I consider every principle in this book to be a truth and applicable in all areas of life. I believe that you will have the same discovery. So whether you are a teacher, parent, corporate executive, coach, grandparent, administrator, doctor, lawyer, cowboy or astronaut I believe that you can find plenty of material to use to improve the quality of your life. I challenge you to challenge yourself and take away some ideas that will improve the quality of your life because this book is all about YOGOWYPI, and You Only Get Out What You Put In!

Bill Cordes

Chapter 1

YOGOWYPI?
YOGOWYPI!

"YOGOWYPI," he whispered.

He then repeated the word, "YOGOWYPI."

The classroom buzzed with snickers. Then with more force and passion, he exclaimed, "YOGOWYPI!"

Dr. Costigan, a tall, thin man who had lost his hair through numerous chemotherapy treatments was speaking volumes. It was not his words that were registering with me, but who he was. Dr. Costigan was my advisor as I pursued my master's degree, and his lectures were always a delight. I had attended many of his classes while getting my undergraduate degree, but I wasn't ready for him at that time. Oh, I loved his classes but I just wasn't ready.

When the Student Is Ready, the Teacher Will Appear

I hadn't struggled enough to understand what Dr. Costigan was saying, and after nearly eight years of working on a bachelor's degree, some soul searching, and two years of teaching high school, I was now ready and thankful that I had the privilege of attending his classes.

"YOGOWYPI," he said, "the measure by which we can evaluate the results we want in life." I was puzzled. What was he talking about? The class was Organizational Communication, and what did YOGOWYPI have to do with anything?

"YOGOWYPI," he said. Dr. Costigan then spoke slowly pausing on each word as if to give us time to come up with the answer before he spilled out the entire message: "You Only Get Out What You…Put In." I chuckled. It made sense.

> *"YOGOWYPI"*
> *"You Only Get Out What You Put In."*
>
> **Dr. Jim Costigan**

His lecture continued, and now it was more directed, more purposeful. His frail body was almost shaking with enthusiasm and passion. Speaking with absolute certainty, he drew us in, paused, and seemed to hold us in the palm of his hand.

"How many times do we walk around with a sense of entitlement…when we have put nothing in?!" he asked and answered at the same time. "We want our relationships to be better, yet we take them for granted. We say we want to be successful, but we are unwilling to risk failure. We say we will work harder if we are paid more, but that's backward thinking. Instead, work harder first. Treat people better first. Exhaust yourself. Exhaust your efforts, and then, regardless of the material gains you have received, you will have gained. Why? Because you had put forth the effort. You had challenged yourself. You had stretched your mind. You had discovered what you are capable of. Then, and only then, you will know the rewards of your service. You only go through this life once, and you only get out what you put into it!"

Thinking about his message, I left class and went to the ATM to get cash so I could buy some groceries. I put the card into the ATM, and pushed *withdrawal from checking* and waited for my 40 dollars to come out of the cash slot. Instead of cash, I received a slip of paper that said, *insufficient funds*.

I slammed my fist to the counter, and thought how unfair this was. I felt victimized by the system. How was I going to get groceries? How was I expected to eat? That was when I caught myself. I did feel that I was entitled. I expected too much for the effort I was putting into my life. My problem wasn't a lack of desire, but it was this sense of entitlement. I had no right to be angry at the world. The world was teaching me a valuable lesson, and I was overdrawn. If I was to get my life in order, I was going to have to take inventory of what I was putting in.

Dr. Costigan was right. I wanted to be successful in the world. I wanted to live a life that mattered. I wanted to make a contribution, yet I was unwilling to take a look at what I was putting in. I wanted everything that was good, but I was unwilling to put forth the effort.

Why Don't We Want to Put Forth the Effort?

When speaking to groups, I always ask for volunteers. It is amazing to watch people respond. I can always predict the response depending upon the age group with whom I am working. When I ask kindergarten students, the air is filled with hands bursting with enthusiasm with the thought of being able to participate. When I ask fifth- and sixth-grade students, about half the students will slowly raise their hands. When I ask high school students, they usually volunteer the person sitting next to them. And when I ask adult groups, no one raises their hands. They fold their arms as if to say, "Not on your life. I learned a long time ago, *never* to volunteer."

How did this happen? We must have all had some common experience that affected our attitude toward being involved. It began in our early years of education when, at some point, the person in the front of the room asked for a volunteer. Someone came to the front of the room, and the teacher asked him or her a question. This person may have been one of us or a friend of ours, but regardless of who it was, this was a defining moment for us. The teacher asked a really tough question, like what is the answer to 1+1, and this person paused, squirmed, and a horrified look came over his or her face. Then came the response. "Elmer's Glue?" Of course, the entire class laughed.

Although we may not remember this moment consciously or specifically, it is etched in our subconscious, and it will never be forgotten. We learned a valuable lesson: "If you don't single yourself out, and if you don't take the risk, then people will not laugh at you."

This is what conditioning is. Conditioning is part of all of our lives, and it is part of the learning process. Advertisers know this. Advertisers spend millions of dollars each year attempting to condition us to believe that if we buy their products, we'll turn out a certain way. Conditioning is so prevalent that the moment we see an ad or hear a jingle, we can automatically identify the product being sold. You may even be able to sing the tune even if you don't use the product. Not only does the conditioning of a culture affect the way we think, but it also affects the way we act. And the media is not the only element of our society that conditions us.

Many of us have conditioned ourselves to get by with as little effort as possible. Why? Because we may fear that if we put in too much effort, we will single ourselves out. This singling out opens us up for ridicule because at that moment of standing up, we are now in the position to be judged by others.

To keep this from happening, many of us have conditioned ourselves into the path of least resistance. We have conditioned ourselves into living a life free of risk, ridicule, and hardship. However, since this path is safe, it also requires little effort. By con-

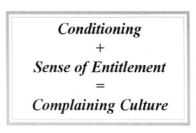

Conditioning
+
Sense of Entitlement
=
Complaining Culture

ditioning ourselves to live with little effort, we also diminish the amount of returns and rewards we could receive. Add that to a sense of entitlement, and we've created a culture that complains a lot about how they didn't get what they deserved.

When We Take Responsibility, We Tap into Our Power

We are all born into a group of people who has been preconditioned. Our parents, teachers, and our community have already been conditioned before we even arrived on the planet. We develop patterns of behavior based upon how we have been preconditioned, and it is difficult to see life differently.

Learned conditioning is somewhat similar to being preconditioned, but there is a difference. That difference is responsibility. When we take responsibility that we learned our negative behaviors because we are so easily conditioned, then we acknowledge that we have the power to change our patterns.

OUR PAST DOES NOT EQUAL OUR FUTURE!

If we believe that we are easily conditioned, then it is true that our past does not equal our future. You and I are not animals. We are thinking people with the ability to recondition our patterns of behavior. Awareness is the first step in making the change. The second step is realizing that you are exactly where you are because of what you have put into your life.

You Have What You Gave

How are your relationships? What does your future hold? How confident are you? What is the state of your finances? How is your family? How is your physical condition? How is your mental and emotional health?

These are all inventory questions, and in order for you to move forward, you need to answer these honestly. You have in life what you gave. End of story. Own it and move forward from this point. Yes, you have been conditioned, but now you are aware of where you are and that you are in control of where you are going next.

This book is about taking inventory where you are now and asking the question: "What have I put in?" The best way to discover what you have put in is to look at what you have created around you. This can be very sobering. But don't stop there. Take a look at what you have and what you have put in. Then ask yourself if you are feeling entitled to something that you don't deserve.

I automatically got mad at the world when there was no money in the ATM. My conditioning told me to get mad, and I looked for someone to blame. We all know that there was no one to blame but me. I believe that all areas of our life are exactly like this. Relationships, businesses, our financial status, and our physical health all go bad because of what we put in. Yes, some things are out of our control, but if we focus our energy on what we have done to create our current situation, this gives us the power to change what we are going to do next.

YOGOWYPI UNIVERSITY

What expectations do you have about college life?

Is it possible that many of those images may be society's rendition of what college is supposed to be?

Other than a diploma, what do you expect to get out of your college experience? Who are you becoming? Are you putting enough in to get what you expect out of your college experience?

Who benefits the most, the person who has their college paid for and can focus solely on their studies, or the person who has to work during college so they can afford to be there? How does your answer fit into the YOGOWYPI equation?

How are your relationships with your family, friends, work associates? Are you the type of person to make the first effort to make those relationships even better, or will you wait for them to take the first step? Regardless of your answer why do you think you are that way? Which strategy gives the most long-term benefit and why?

How much does building relationships play into the total college experience?

The **YOGOWYPI** *Review !*

YOGOWYPI = YOU ONLY GET OUT WHAT YOU PUT IN!

Have you been putting enough in to live the life you expect?

Often times we condition ourselves out of being involved in our own lives.

It is important to re-condition ourselves so that we take full responsibility.

You have in life what you have given. Could you give more?

YOGOWYPI Rule #1:
It is better to pay the
price than to get it for
free...

CHAPTER 2

YOGOWYPI:
The Message Behind the Simple Truth

You may have chuckled as I did when you saw the title of this book. Maybe you heard someone say "YOGOWYPI," and agreed that you only get out what you put in. It seems so simple, yet the meaning is deep. All of the great truths are like that. They're simple, yet hidden in their simplicity is a much deeper message.

YOGOWYPI is a simple truth, and here are a few of the deeper messages hidden within this truth. In addition to the eight components of YOGOWYPI, this book will show you the key strategies for getting past your conditioning and into a life that works.

YOGOWYPI is based upon eight components. Each component is defined by the letters of YOGOWYPI, and the next ten chapters each explore these components in depth. Here is a brief overview of these eight components:

Y = You Choose Your Approach

There are some things in life that we consciously choose. There are some things that we unconsciously choose. Then there are some things in life that we don't choose at all. If something shows up in your life, it doesn't matter whether you chose it or not. What matters is what you do next. What will you do with the things that show up in your life?

This book is about making the best choice no matter what circumstance you find yourself in. It's about taking a solid analysis of what is in your life at this very moment and making the best choice about how to deal with it.

We can all sit around and feel guilty about the events of the 17th century. We can agonize over these events and wish that things would have been different. But, we will never change the outcome of those events.

Yesterday is just as gone as the 17th century. We can't change our childhood. We can't change the family we were born into, and we can't change yesterday. We can wish certain things wouldn't have happened, but we will never change these things. We can feel guilty about some of the things we have done, but we can't change that either. We cannot change the past.

But there is something we can change. We can change what we do about what is happening to us right now. The one thing we have control over is the present! So this book is about releasing yourself from your past and helping you choose your approach to your life right now. Choosing an approach will not change your past, but it will change the past of your future. You can set in motion a new series of choices that will lead you toward a more productive future as well as a new past that you will be proud of.

O = O-Zone

The O-zone is a circle filled with our experiences. Based

on our experiences, we have developed certain attitudes about change and safety. We all want comfort and stability, but when we aim for those things, we often stop taking risks. As we understand our O-zone, it will become easier to develop healthier attitudes toward change as well as understanding why we refuse to change. Our past patterns can defeat us, and we can move past those patterns by focusing on big picture thinking and creating success.

G = Great Efforts Yield Great Results

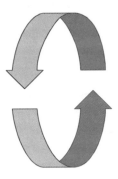

The law of the "put in" says that little effort brings little results and great effort yields great results. Understanding the law helps us understand why we have in life what we have. It also supports us in learning where we can place our efforts in order to maximize our benefits. You will learn key distinctions that will support you in understanding the keys for gaining the most out of your efforts. As we place our attention in the right place, we can achieve the optimal mindset for producing positive results.

O = O₂–The Key Element for Success

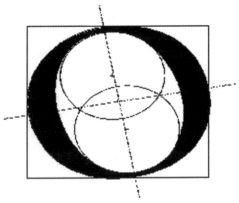

The one essential element for life is O_2. Oxygen not only is essential for life, it also is essential for positive growth. Just as oxygen is necessary for life, responsibility is necessary to sustain our healthy life choices. Unfortunately, a lot of us believe certain myths about responsibility. (We have been negatively conditioned about its true meaning.) There's a new, useful paradigm for responsibility, and this insight can help us create a more joyful, productive life.

W = Wisdom of Mission

To design a compelling, productive future, we need to know three things. First: We need to know where we are. Second, we need to know what we are doing. And third, we need to know why we are doing what we are doing. Wisdom of mission teaches us to tap into our most creative self so we will have the drive to work hard. This is all about understanding ourselves and what drives us. We've all seen people who have passion and a burning desire for living a life that matters. We're going to find out what these people have and begin using their wisdom.

Y = Y₂Learn

The learning game is the one that excites me the most because so many of us have bought into the belief that learning is dull, tedious, and unfulfilling. Certain barriers keep us from learning. By adopting helpful concepts, we can all develop an insatiable appetite for learning and apply new strategies in our lives. Ongoing success is impossible unless we recondition ourselves to have a healthy view of learning. Y₂ Learn contains the necessary elements for moving past failure and into the learning zone. It spells out how to use exciting learning tools that can transform your memory, your retention, and your ability to synthesize large pieces of information in a short period of time.

P = People Are "People-People" by Design

People are your greatest resource. Without the support of the people you love, your path toward success will result in disappointment and failure. Certain communication strategies help you to enlist the support of others as well empower yourself in the face of adversity. What tears relationships apart? These are the sand traps we want to avoid. As we find out how to build teamwork, unity, and trust in people, we will acquire the strategies for building a lifelong network of people that matter.

I = Integration

You can either know about something or you can actually know it. Knowing about something just makes it an acquaintance to you, but when you really know it, then it becomes a part of you. In order for the YOGOWYPI factor to take hold in your life, you must integrate these concepts into your daily life. This won't happen unless you practice the skills in this book and use the tools on a consistent basis day by day. This book includes strategies for making these skills a regular part of your life so that when you really need these skills, you will be ready. And when you're skilled, ready, and putting in a great amount of effort, you will create the life that you really want.

YOGOWYPI UNIVERSITY

Whatever you can do
Or dream you can
Begin it.
Boldness has genius,
power and magic in it!
BEGIN IT NOW!
GOETHE

Today, my father called and wanted to help out a friend of his who was interested in finding an adult child whom he had not seen in many years. For whatever reason they had lost contact, and now he decided to make things better by renewing this relationship. I got a few pieces of information, spent ten minutes on the internet, found the number, and called my dad. Because my dad's friend was bold enough to ask for help he is well on his way to making his life, and his daughter's life better. *Boldness has genius, power and magic in it! Begin it now!*

This book is about boldness and taking action, and the bottom line is you don't need this book to make your life better, but you do need to put something in if you want to improve the quality of your life. Class is now in session, and you will be gaining the tools, but before you do anything else be bold and take action. Your first course at YOGOWYPI U. is to take a personal action that would improve the quality of your life.

What is the one positive behavior I could eliminate, change or begin that would make my life better?

You already know what the answer is, and you have plenty of excuses as to why you have not made the change now. So why not begin it now? You could wait five, ten or fifteen years to make that change, but just know the longer you wait the tougher it is to change. The quality of your life depends upon the positive actions you take, and the amount of value you receive while attending YOGOWYPI U. depends on it! Your action may be small or huge, but whatever you do it must improve the quality of your life. Write your action statement on the bottom of this page, and begin the process of putting more in, so you can receive greater rewards right...**NOW!**

Write your first specific, short-term action statement here:

BEGIN IT NOW!

The YOGOWYPI Review!

Y = You Choose Your Approach

O = O-zone

G = Great Efforts Yield Great Rewards

O = O_2 Oxygen: Responsibility Makes It Work

W = Wisdom of Mission

Y = Y_2Learn

P = People Are "People-People" by Design

I = Integrate

Chapter 3
Y = You Choose Your Approach!

I laid awake in a cold sweat, worrying and wondering what I was going to do with my life. I felt that all my life choices up to this point had been wrong. I was 25 years old, and I was in my seventh year of college. Graduation from this institution seemed nowhere in sight. It looked like I needed to drop two more classes that semester because I didn't want two more Fs on my college transcript, which was already looking like a long list of failures.

I thought about those who were already out of college and starting their careers. I felt like I just did not get it, and I knew there was something wrong with me. I got out of bed, went to the bathroom, and stared into the mirror. It was 4 a.m., and I was going nowhere.

All my worrying only made this bad situation worse. I had felt like this many times before, and I knew that college was the right place for me. The problem wasn't the choices I had made. The problem was my approach to my choices.

This was an almost-typical night for me in college. I was okay on the outside, but on the inside, I was in the middle of the most worrisome period of my life. Luckily for me, I had a friend who understood my troubles. One day during lunch, she told me about a seminar that she had taken. I asked her what it was, and she simply said it was a class on life.

"Well, how much does it cost?" I asked.

"450 dollars," she replied.

"450 dollars?" I laughed. The price could have been 450 thousand dollars, and it would have been the same. I was a struggling college student, and that was a lot of money. I had never had 450 dollars in my bank account. I was poor. I had always been poor, and I knew that there was no way I could find that kind of money.

Then she said, "Well 450 is only for the first class. The second class, which I highly recommend, is 1,000 dollars. And the third is 400 dollars. I think you should attend all three of them. It would do you a lot of good."

I continued to laugh, and she said, "It is a total of 1,850 dollars. I know it sounds like a lot now, but the question you should be asking is this: What is your life worth to you?"

What Is Your Life Worth?

Have you thought about it? What are you willing to give up right now to make your life better? Only you can decide the value of your own life, and you can survive. The question, however, is: Do you just want to survive, or are your expectations higher than that?

I am not going to ask you to spend 1,850 dollars as you read this book. My price is even higher. I am going to ask for your time and your commitment. Yes, I took all three  classes, and yes, they were worth every penny I invested. But the reason these classes were worth so much for me was because I invested everything I had into them.

Since then, I have received my investment back thousands of times over, and it continues to be a wonderful ride. The truth is, what I paid for those classes was a fraction of what I paid for my entire college career. The difference was how I approached these three classes. I was rigorous with myself. I was determined to make changes. It was time

> *If I am trading a day of my life for what I put in today, am I getting a good deal?*

for me to make my life matter, and I knew that if I didn't make some changes now, I only would be putting off what I eventually would need to put in.

There Is Another Way

What I discovered as my journey unfolded was that there is another way. I had been living my life out of scarcity, fear of failure, and worrying about what could happen. What I failed to see was the world of possibility and opportunity.

A few years ago, I bought a Lincoln Mark VIII, and I really liked the car. It seemed like the perfect car for all of my long trips. Then one night while cruising the Web, I came  across a Web site created for Mark VIII owners. I was astounded that people were absolutely nuts about how much they enjoyed their car. As I read the postings, I noticed a lot of people talking about headlamp replacements and how much they enjoyed their new high-intensity discharge headlamps. They claimed these headlamps made a huge difference when they drove at night.

I purchased the headlights, and I had them installed. On my first trip, I had an amazing discovery. Eureka! I hadn't known what I was missing. What a difference! I could see things I had never seen before. It was like a whole world opened up to me. The lows cast a much more even-il-luminated beam, and the high beams seemed to stretch for miles. I not only could see what was in front of me bet-ter, but the peripheries made it seem

> *Do you know what you are not seeing?*

like I was driving in daylight. Had I not come across that Web site, I would have been fine with my old headlamps.

Now that I have the new ones, I would never go back.

It is hard to know what you are missing, if you can't see what you are missing. Is it possible that you have been driving with the wrong headlights? What if you could discover another way of seeing that allowed you to see ahead of you in a brighter, clearer, more-focused way? If that were possible, would it be worth investing everything you have into finding this new way?

Not Choosing Is Choosing

I had been driving around with the wrong headlights, and I hadn't realized that I had made that choice. My problem was not my ability or that I was in the wrong place. My problem was that I refused to choose how to approach my life situation.

By not choosing, I was making a choice. Because I hadn't chosen, I wasn't working hard enough to decide what I wanted out of the circumstances I was in. We can all choose the path we want to take, but along with that path we also must choose an approach to guide us on our path because...

It Is Your Approach that Makes the Difference

Craig Hillier (friend, mentor, and fellow professional speaker) and I have spent hours discussing the one essential component that makes the biggest difference in gaining life's grandest rewards. What we have discovered is that it is our approach that makes the difference. Together we have had more than a million people attend our programs, and we wish we could say that everyone left our programs totally ready to embrace life with new meaning.

But that isn't true. We did our part, but not everyone who came to our programs did theirs.

The reality is that we could attend the greatest seminar in the world, but if we approached the program with the wrong perspective, we wouldn't gain the maximum value. This is true with all of life's endeavors. We can attend the best school, be on the best team, work for the best company, and have the greatest family. But those things alone won't bring us what we want. It is not life's circumstances that produce life's great rewards, but it is our approach to life's circumstances that gives life value. It is not what you have or where you are. It is what you do with what you have been given.

In my seminars, I ask a number of people to stand around me in a large group. Using a beach ball, I ask these people how many times they can hit the ball consecutively without the ball hitting the ground. I say that each person can hit the ball only one time, and after a person hits the ball, he or she must kneel to represent that his or her turn has been taken.

It's not what you have or where you are, but it's what you do with what you have been given that really matters.

During the first round, the group may have achieved 10 consecutive hits. Then I ask the group to set a goal. Everyone stands up, and we repeat the activity until the goal is reached. Everyone is jubilant. They reached the goal!

Then I ask a series of questions about what the game was designed to teach us. I usually get the standard answers like teamwork, goal setting, and communication. Then

I ask if anyone noticed what happened to the group's energy level as the group got closer to the goal. Most people say, "We got excited. We worked harder, and we started to have more fun."

Then I ask, "Do you think your approach made any difference?" Naturally, everyone agrees that the group's attitude was essential. Then we talk about our approach to life and how it makes all the difference in the world in creating future success.

Leaners, Lookers, and Leaders

Craig Hillier and I have surmised that there are three different approaches to what life deals us. These three approaches determine the amount of value that we can receive from any challenge, problem or opportunity.

You choose your approach every moment of every day. However, most of us walk around not realizing that we are choosing our approach. We walk around on automatic pilot, assuming that things happen to us, rather than realizing that our approach is what has led us into a particular circumstance.

We take on challenges based upon one of three approaches. These aren't personality styles; they're approaches. All of us have used each of these three approaches at one time or another.

Approach #1: The Leaner

Some of us start an activity or a situation with the leaner approach. We may ask: "Do we have to do this?" "What

does this have to do with this class?" Or we may comment how stupid it is or irrelevant it is. Leaners usually approach life from a have-to perspective. Unless it was their idea, then someone is making them do something.

Leaners see very little choice in their day-to-day activities. They go to school because they have to. They go to work because they have to. They pay bills because they have to. They go to family reunions because they have to. They see life as a series of problems, and they seldom want to come up with any solutions, except to complain. They are critical of their assignments and projects, and they don't see any redeeming value in working hard.

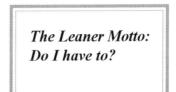

The Leaner Motto:
Do I have to?

Approach #2: The Looker

The looker approach is somewhat different. Lookers are slightly open, and they will get involved only if it looks safe. Lookers are not totally resistant, yet they are not totally involved. Lookers often will choose involvement if they see others gaining value. Their approach to life is "hope to." Lookers will say things like, "I hope this seminar is good." "I hope this class is not going to be boring." "I sure hope everything goes okay this week."

Now I believe in hope, and I believe hope is a good thing to have. But lookers mean something different when they talk about hope. Their hope suggests that they really don't have any control. They are looking for luck. They're hoping that they will get lucky, and things will go their way.

> *The looker relies on "hope" rather than action.*

Lookers can be dreamers, but they get lost on the island of "someday I'll...." When it comes down to it, lookers will not work hard enough to get the job done unless they are lucky and good fortune smiles upon them.

Lookers differ from leaners in that they will get involved if things are going well. In the seminar world, lookers check out the room. If they see that others are having fun, they will choose to get involved as well. In the student world, lookers test the waters. If they discover that others are having fun learning, then they'll learn something too. In the work world, lookers love to be on the winning team. If they see that a project has promise, they will get involved and push it through to the end. However, if they see the possibility of failure, lookers will avoid the responsibility like the plague. In short, lookers are fair-weather fans who make it their goal to be on the winning team because they see it as an opportunity to look like winners without having to risk the possibility of failure.

Approach #3: The Leader

The leader will create value in any situation. Leaders understand that life has optimal situations and ones that are less than positive. However, leaders choose not to leave the possible value they could receive to chance. A leader says, "Since I am here, I will make it valuable. My input will make a difference."

While lookers and leaners search for ways to be entertained, leaders jump in to create value with what they are given. The motto in life for leaders is not "have to" or "hope to" but "want to" and "get to."

Ask leaders about challenges in their life, and they will tell you how they are trying to solve them. Ask leaders about school, and they will tell you the classes and projects that excite them. Leaders are rare, but wherever they go, they make an impact because they leave nothing to chance. Even in the worst possible situation, leaders will leave that situation knowing they are richer because of it.

Leaders are open to everything but attached to nothing. They view the world as full of possibilities and choose not to cling to people needing to be a certain way. They understand that everything will not go their way. They know that everyone will not agree with their position. The interesting thing

> *Leaders will create value in any situation.*

about leaders, however, is that you always know where you stand with them and that they are not afraid of being wrong.

Leaders are not leaders because they want to look good, but because they want the group to produce results. They are not standing around hoping that the lesson, the event, or the project will be valuable. Instead, they assert that their contribution will make it valuable.

Your Approach

How do you change your approach? The answer isn't simply about changing your language. Instead, it's the process of applying the contents of this book. It begins by asserting that *you choose*. When you choose your approach and apply the attributes of the YOGOWYPI factor, you will steer your life in a different direction. You'll have the high-intensity headlamps that will light your way.

YOGOWYPI UNIVERSITY

Did you complete your mission from chapter two?

If not then don't do anything else until you have completed your mission. It is very important to the content of chapter three that you complete your mission of taking a specific action to improve your life.

Describe your life approach. Are you predominantly a leaner, looker or leader? Remember, this has little to do with your personality style, but more to do with how you approach life situations.

Describe a situation that may cause you to take a "leaner" approach.

Describe a situation that may cause you to take a "looker" approach.

Describe a situation that may cause you to take on a "leader" approach.

What is the difference that causes you to change your approach?

Have you ever started out with one approach and then changed? What caused you to change?

The **YOGOWYPI** *Review!*

*You choose! It is the approach you choose that makes the difference.

*What is your life worth? What would you spend to improve the quality of your life?

*There is another way. Is it possible to see your life in a way that would cause you to work harder and put more into making your life better? What are you not seeing?

*It is our approach that makes the difference.

*The three approaches are: Leaners, Lookers and Leaders.

*Leaners feel as if the world is forcing itself upon them and that they are "victimized" by society.

*Lookers will get involved if they feel comfortable and it looks good to them.

*Leaders will create value in any situation. They know that they will find a way to make any situation valuable.

The O-Zone

Chapter 4
O = O-Zone

Imagine a brand new oak desk has been delivered to you. As you admire the fine craftsmanship, take a second and ponder the state of your desk. Is your desk in the state of growth, stability or decay? Most people would look at the desk and say, "It is very solid. Therefore, it must be in the state of stability."

What if you had the ability to check your desk two hundred years from now. What would you say then? You probably would notice that it has decayed slightly. So that leads to my next question: "Isn't it in that state right now?" Sure it is. We got caught by the illusion of stability. Even though this is about a desk, we as people are the same way....

Stability Does Not Exist

We are either green and growing or decaying and dying. There is no in between. Stability does not exist!

Our language attempts to lure us into the illusion that

stability does exist. People ask, "How are you?" We say, "fine." What does that mean? Are we stable? I guess saying that we're fine is better than saying, "You know, I am really decaying today. I am falling apart."

The first time we dated someone seriously, we called it going steady. Now how stable was that? Our parents tell us to get out and get both feet on the ground. In other words, they are telling us to find stability.

Does that ever really happen? No. It never happens. We are either striving to find new heights or slipping down a slope. We are either discovering more about ourselves or we're not finding anything at all. We are either learning, growing and expanding our limits or we are simply decaying.

Socrates, said it best: "The only constant in the universe is change."

> *The only constant in the universe is change.*
> **Socrates**

If change is the only constant, then the one thing that we can always be assured of as people is that we are either in a state of growth or in a state of decay. How do you

know which one is true for you right now? The answer lies in your O-zone.

Examining Your O-Zone

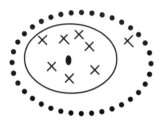

We all have an O-zone. Our O-zone is a circle filled with our experiences. Our first experience out in the world, represented by the dot in the center of the circle, was birth. From there, we had a variety of experiences, represented by the x's inside the circle. We learned to talk, walk, ride a bike, go to school, have relationships, struggle, succeed, and fail.

We are more comfortable with the things on the inside of our O-zone than we are with the things on the outside of our O-zone. That's because we *know* all the things on the inside of our O-zone. Anything outside our O-zone is unknown.

If we do things that we have always done, our lives become very comfortable. That's the good news. The bad news about comfort is that our lives also get very boring. We become like a pool of water that has no fresh water feed. We begin to stagnate. Thus the O-zone becomes our comfort zone, our boredom zone, our stagnation zone and our decay zone.

Doing new things leads to growth. Experiences on the outside of our O-zone may make us feel uncomfortable, and we may feel shaky as if we are standing on new territory. But this feeling of discomfort has rewards in and of itself. This feeling of stretching beyond what is known leads us into the growth zone.

Understanding the Great Paradox

Given the choice, most of us would choose comfort over discomfort. Most of us also would choose growth over stagnation. This brings us to a great paradox. We like being comfortable, but we don't want to decay. We want to grow, but we dislike being uncomfortable.

What's the solution? We need to move past the fear of immediate discomfort and get excited about who you will become after you have conquered each portion of your O-zone. Go beyond your natural tendency and strive for discomfort. After all, discomfort is the only way we know for sure that we are growing.

Am I saying that we should do everything outside of our comfort zone? Absolutely not. Otherwise we would have people jumping off of large buildings yelling, "I am going outside of my comfort zooooonnnnneeeee!" This is where you need to tap into your wisdom. You need to know which kind of discomfort will serve you in the long run. It is knowing the difference between the big picture and the little picture.

The Big Picture Versus the Little Picture

Notice the picture. What captures your attention? You may see a large picture of space with a frame around it. As

you look at this picture of nothingness, it is almost impossible not to notice the small frame down in the corner. In fact, the more I ask you to focus on the big picture, the more your eye will be drawn to the smaller picture.

Life is like that. We get so caught up in the small picture that we fail to see the endless possibilities of the big picture.

Take Lisa, for example. Lisa had been working as an account executive for nearly seven years. She was very good at her job, and she was pleased with her ability to move up the ladder in her company. Yet, as she looked down the road in her career, she didn't get very excited about what was possible in her future. Her pay was adequate, but all she could

> *Often times we get so caught up in the details of the small picture that we fail to see the endless possibilities of the big picture.*

think about was having her own advertising agency. Lisa knew that if she left her job to start up her agency that she would risk failure, money, security and the comfort she had in her current position.

Little-Picture Thinking—Little picture thinking is characterized by fear of what might happen. We notice the big-picture possibilities of what might happen if we take the risk, but the overwhelming fear of failure consumes us and brings our focus back to the little picture of fear, scarcity, and comfort. Our internal dialogue sounds something like this, "I am comfortable with the classes I am taking now." "I'm not taking that class because I heard it's really hard." "What will my friends think if I can't do it?" These fears are real, and we should treat them as such. Remember, it is not necessary to take every risk that comes along, but in order to have growth in life we must take necessary risk or we will stagnate.

Big-Picture Thinking—It's more helpful to ask better questions, such as: "If I did fail, how much would I grow as a result of the failure?" "If I stayed in my current, comfortable classes, would I look back at that as a failure?" "What would I do if I knew that failure was not an option? Wouldn't I be better off making the attempt?"

Big-picture thinking acknowledges the option of failure, but it also places the focus on the possibility of what might happen rather than on the small frame of immediate gratification. When we are thinking in the big picture, we are choosing not to allow the fears that go along with the O-zone. Instead, we choose to trade our immediate fears for the bigger pay-off that comes when we choose to live outside of the O-zone.

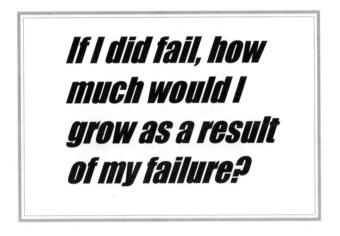

If I did fail, how much would I grow as a result of my failure?

High school English was a tedious time of my life. This wasn't because my teacher wasn't good, but the thought of English in the morning was never something that got my blood flowing. To make things even worse, this old guy taught my class. We called him "Uncle Walt" behind his back.

I didn't know this at the time, but Uncle Walt had actually gone back to college late in life, and he didn't start teaching until he was in his late forties. As I look back on my classes with him, I am sure that is why he was a little different. Uncle Walt, like all good teachers, was a little off his rocker. Each day in the middle of his blackboard, he had written the word *awareness*. He spent much of his time making sure that we understood why that word was such a big part of English class.

After class, we would sometimes mock him. "It's about awareness," we would say. "You have to be aware!" It was a running joke that my friends and I had about Uncle Walt because we thought that we were aware and that he was overstating the obvious. The truth was that Uncle Walt was teaching us that we don't know what awareness was. Now

I know that he was absolutely right. It is about awareness.

Awareness is knowing why you are doing what you are doing. Are we making choices because of little-picture thinking and our desire to live in the O-zone so that we trade-in comfort for growth? Or are we choosing to look at the big picture and making decisions based upon what we want to get out of our life? Are we aware enough to sacrifice the little picture so we can stretch ourselves beyond what we know? Are we making a good trade for the time we are putting into our life?

Be Aware That This Is It

Awareness is the key to understanding that *this is it*. Throughout our entire lives, we have been conditioned into thinking "where we are now is not it." If you don't believe me, just take a look at your life and notice how unaware you have been.

If you had an older brother or sister who went to school before you, then you probably remember sitting at home and wondering what he or she did at school all day. You may have even thought, "I don't want to stay at home anymore because this is *not* it."

On your first day of school, after you got passed the initial nervousness and met your teacher, you probably said, "I made it. I am in school, and *this is it*." As days went by, however, and you became comfortable at school, you started to look around again. Kids in first grade did more than you did in kindergarten, so you concluded that this is not it. First grade must be it. So summer vacation came, and by the end of summer, you were a real big kid, and you got to go to first grade.

A few months into first grade, you figured it out. It isn't first grade, so it must be second grade. The pattern continued until finally you realized that elementary school wasn't it at all. It must be high school.

When you got to high school, it didn't take you long to figure out that high school wasn't it either. College was. I talk to college kids all the time, and they keep telling me that college isn't it. The real world is it. When they get a job and make some money, that will be it.

There are all kinds of people out there in the real world doing their jobs, making money, making a living, and you can guess what they are saying: "This is not it. Retirement. Retirement must be it."

Large numbers of people in our culture live their entire lives thinking that this is not it. They look forward to retirement when they can sit around and talk about the good ol' days, but they never had any because where they were was never it. For these people, I have a simple solution.

This Is It

Where you are now *is it*. Right here, right now. Learn to glean all of life's lessons from each moment. Learn to live each moment, because each moment is it. Plan for the future. Stretch yourself in the moment. Go beyond your O-zone and into the unknown with each passing day. Be aware of why you are doing what you are doing, and gain the wisdom of mission necessary to live a life that truly matters!

YOGOWYPI UNIVERSITY

Stretch: The experience of going beyond the barriers of your O-zone into the uncomfortable zone.

*In chapter two you were challenged to do something that would improve the quality of your life. Did you follow though?

*Rate your stretch on a scale of 1-10. One means I stretched myself by waking up before noon. Ten means I did the emotional equivilant of bungee jumping into fire while eating scorpions.

Rating_____

*How successful were you in your stretch? Did you succeed or fail? By now you are starting to realize that expanding your O-zone is its own reward. However, greater stretches yield greater rewards, which is the topic of chapter 5.

*Your next stretch is to set a specific goal with a timeframe that you will take action on today. Remember, this must be an outcome that the very thought of it brings up the emotion of fear and the possibility of failure. Maybe your outcome is relational, maybe it has to do with getting a job, talking to a professor, declaring a major, or confronting a situation that has been bothering you. Attempting this outcome should stetch your mind, body and imagination!

*What is it that keeps you from stretching yourself?

*What role does the little picture play in keeping you from doing the things that you know could create personal growth?

*What role could the big picture play in getting you to take action?

*Awareness, could be described as a presence in the moment, and an understanding of how every action can contibute to your future. How aware are you? What are some things that you could do daily that would increase your level of life awareness?

THIS IS IT! What are you looking forward to that is keeping you from being present in the moment? Is it graduating from college? Will that be it? What positive life experience are you missing out on by waiting until you graduate? What could you do today that would pave the road for a better life in the future?

What would be different in your life if you fully lived in the moment while planning for the future?

The YOGOWYPI Review!

*Stability is a myth. We are either green and growing or dead and dying. There is no in between.

*To expand your O-zone means to go beyond the comfortable into the realm of new experiences, and doing it wisely.

*Big picture little picture thinking is focusing on the rewards and pleasures of risk rather than the fear of failure. Often times we sell out for the little picture and never get the rewards.

*Awareness is the state of focusing on how our daily actions can affect the big picture.

*This Is It! Plan for the future while being present in the moment. Do today, what will reward you in the future!

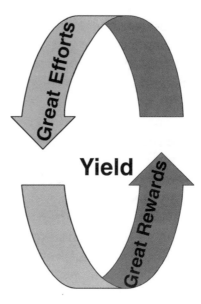

Chapter 5

G = Great Efforts Yield Great Rewards

Jake Porter likes football, and he has been on the team since he was in middle school. During his football career, Jake has never missed a practice. He has suited up for nearly every game, but he has never had the chance to play in an actual football game.

You see, even though Jake Porter loves football, it was too risky for the coach to allow him to play because Jake Porter suffers from chromosomal fragile X syndrome, a disorder that is a common cause of mental retardation. Even though Jake has never played in a football game, he is well known throughout the area as an athlete who gives his best. In the past, he has participated in track meets and basketball games, but he never had the chance to play in a football game, the sport he loves most dearly.

To understand Jake, you must first understand the kind of person he is and what the students of Ohio's Northwest High School think of him. Jake is very popular, but it isn't because of his ability. It is because of his good nature and willingness to support others by just being a part of the team.

Jake helps out the coaching staff, cleans up after practice, and participates in all the drills during practice that are not too risky for his ability. Jake is widely accepted at Northwest High School and has the kind of energy that simply draws people to him.

With five seconds remaining in Jake's last game of his senior year, Northwest was down 42-0. Northwest's Coach Dave Frantz called a time out. Coach Franz wanted to ask opposing Head Coach Derek Dewitt if it was okay if Jake came into the game, received the ball, and then took a knee. Coach Franz simply wanted Jake to be able to say that he played in a high school football game.

Coach Dewitt disagreed. He thought Jake should not take a knee. Instead he wanted Jake to run 49 yards and score a touchdown. Coach Franz, was overwhelmed. "We had talked about it the day before about letting Porter take a knee," he said, "but we never thought [Coach] Derek [Dewitt] would do this."

Prior to the play, Jake was told not to take a knee as they had practiced but instead to "go all the way to the big house." Coach Frantz said that Jake was grinning ear to ear as he took the field.

Jake received the hand off and started to take a knee when teammates stopped him and told him to run. Jake started to run in the wrong direction, but the referee stopped him and turned Jake in the right direction. As Jake ran toward the line of scrimmage, players parted to give Jake

> *Prior to the play, Jake was told not to take a knee as they had practiced but instead to "go all the way to the big house."*

room. Then they turn and ran with Jake the entire 49 yards to the goal line.

Fathers and mothers in the stands cried and cheered. Players from both teams held their helmets high. Afterward, Jake's mom, Liz, ran up to Coach Frantz to thank him but was so overrun with emotion that she was unable to speak. Coach Dewitt was so excited that you would have never known that he gave up his first ever coaching shut out to give Jake a chance to score a touchdown.

Great Efforts Yield Great Rewards

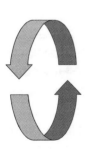

Jake was given this opportunity because both Jake and Coach Frantz understood that *great efforts yield great results*. For years, Jake had been a part of the team. His contribution had been so great that Coach Frantz wanted to do more for the kid who had given so much.

Jake Porter didn't come to all those years of practice because he knew that he would get the opportunity to run for a touchdown during his senior year. Jake served and contributed because he understood that great efforts are their own rewards. For six years, Jake was allowed to be a part of middle- and high-school football, and for Jake, that was reward enough. However, great things come to those who contribute because they *want to* and not because they *have to*.

The Law of the Put In

Years ago when I was single, I was visiting my mother for the holidays. My 10-year-old niece, Sara, asked, "Uncle Bill when are you going home?"

I said, "I am leaving today because I get to go to work on Monday."

As I left the room, I heard Sara ask my Mom. "Grandma, did Uncle Bill say he gets to go to work on Monday?"

My mother responded, "Well, yes he did."

A long pause followed before my niece finally spoke up and asked, "Doesn't he have to go?"

My mother, and bless her heart for her infinite wisdom and wit in explaining things, said, "Sara, I think it is time you understood something about your Uncle Bill. He is not like a lot of people. He is a little different. He likes his job, so he says he gets to go to work!"

In all fairness to my mother, she is right. I am a little different, but my job at the time was not anymore special to me than other jobs I had worked in at that time. However, thanks to Dr. Costigan, I understood the *law of the put in.*

The Law of the Put In says that if you *have to* do something, then you don't get to receive the rewards of your efforts. So in the YOGOWYPI formula, the *have to* negates the *put in*, which lessens the *get out*. The more you feel you *have to* do something, the *fewer* rewards you'll receive for your efforts.

Something to Think about

I *have to* go to work until I *want to* go to work. Then I don't *have to* go to work anymore.

I often say this in my seminars to see how participants will respond. I repeat it several times, and then ask, "What does it mean?"

I usually get responses like, "It means that if you do your work well then you will find better opportunities."

Eventually, after a period of silence, someone says, "It is a statement about attitude. If you feel that you *want to* do something, then it is not an obligation, but a choice."

> *I have to go to work until I want to go to work then I don't have to go to work anymore.*

Jake Porter never felt that being involved with the football team was a *have to,* even though many of his responsibilities were a lot of work, and Jake never received any of the glory that was associated with game time until that very last game. Jake simply did what he did because he enjoyed making a contribution to the team. For him that was enough.

When we act like the Jake Porters of the world, our life actions feel like choices instead of obligations. When we remove the *have to's* from our life, we recondition ourselves to not be victims.

What Makes You a Victim

Victimization is learned, and spotting a victim takes about 30 seconds. Just pay attention to the language patterns of victims. Victims *have to* do a lot of things. They *have to* go to class. They *have to* go to work. They *have to* pick up their children. They *have to* pay their bills, and *they have* to spend time with their families. Somewhere they learned that if they *have to* do something, then they will get some sort of pay off from others.

If someone *has to* do something, then he or she becomes a victim of circumstance. But victims aren't just helpless people. Many victims have just displaced their put-in efforts.

Look at how victimization works. Others may help victims or feel sorry for all of the things victims *have to* do. Since victims *have to* do something, then they are saying that someone, or some situation, is *making* them do it. Then whoever is *making* them do it, gets the credit. That other person, or that other situation, gets the *put in* for the efforts of a victim, and a victim becomes a victim because that other person, or that other circumstance, *made* the victim.

Want to is a whole different scenario. *Want to* asserts choice. If I am responding to my world based on choice, then I am not the victim but the victor, and I get to reap the rewards of my put in.

Make the shift so you can *get out* of your life what you *put into* it. Take the *have to* out of your vocabulary, and speak as a chooser: a person with power who is controlling his or her own destiny. Instead of *have to,* use *want to* and *get to*. Want tos give you power because they communicate choice.

Strive to Do More than Simply Getting By

As my friend Michael sat down to take his first college class, Philosophy 101, the professor showed up and started explaining his expectations for the class. The professor announced, "I have been teaching this class for many years, and I know exactly what is going to happen as we proceed through the semester. Some of you are going to move to the front of the class. You are going to get involved in the lectures, do the readings, and participate in the discussion. You will get more out of this class than your grade. You will get an education.

"Some of you are taking the class because your advisor told you that you must take philosophy in order to graduate. So, I am going to make a deal with you. If you show up for my class everyday, you can do whatever you want while you are here. You can sit in the back, read the newspaper, listen to a Walkman, or even sleep. If you are here everyday, I will guarantee you a C."

A student in the class raised his hand and asked, "You mean, all we have to do is attend class everyday, and you will give us a C?"

"That's right," the professor said.

Someone else raised her hand and asked, "What's the catch?"

"There is no catch," the professor replied. "You and I live in an abundant culture that is filled with opportunities. We live in a world where we can pretty

Is simply getting by enough?

much just show up and just get by. The question is: Who wants to just get by?"

Mistakes Are Great Moments

In my *Great Moments* seminar, I teach juggling to businesses, service groups, students and leaders. I start by taking three balls and begin to juggle. I then inform the participants that by the end of the session, every person in this room will learn how to juggle. Then I immediately stop and ask participants to write what they're thinking about what I just said in the workshop notes titled *Internal Dialogue #1.*

I tell them that sugar coating is not necessary. I want people's honest internal dialogue about what they think is their ability to learn to juggle during the session. Then I have participants share what they wrote with the group.

Most people are very negative in their approach to learning to juggle. I get responses like, "I have tried juggling before, and I couldn't do it." "I am uncoordinated, and I can't learn," and "It is not going to happen."

Next, I take participants through a process that teaches them to celebrate their mistakes because *mistakes are great moments.* I explain that if participants can put in effort without any judgment and have at least 100 *great moments* throughout this session, they *will* learn to juggle.

By the time we end learning about two-ball juggling, the resistance has diminished. By the time we get to three-ball juggling, hundreds of people are walking around celebrating their great moments and learning to juggle.

Feedback Is the Breakfast of Champions

If I have the proper timeframe to teach juggling, I have 90+% success rate. Even those who don't get it will admit with a little extra time and effort they could learn.

How can people go from *no way* to *I'll find a way* in such a short period of time? The answer lies in the *permission to fail*. Everyone has the ability to learn, but people can only learn if they are willing to have 100 great moments.

Each great moment puts you closer to your goal. Each time you fail, evaluate your effort and mark your attempt as feedback. The more feedback you receive from yourself about what works and what doesn't work, the closer you will get to achieving your goal.

At the end of my juggling workshop, I remind participants about the lack of confidence they had in the beginning and ask them to note how quickly they turned it around. I ask, "Obviously today was not about learning to juggle, so what was it about?"

I usually get the following responses: "Learn to commit yourself to something even though you might fail." "Mistakes are great moments." "Believe in yourself and learn to shut out negative internal dialogue." "If we are willing to put in the effort, we can move past our own limiting beliefs."

I then ask: "If at the beginning of this session you believed you couldn't juggle, and now you can juggle, then where else in your life are you holding yourself back?"

My question for you is the same: "Where in your life are you holding yourself back because you are unwilling to put in the effort and move past the failure?"

Jake Porter put in the effort. He put in years of effort. He was willing to sit on the bench for every game through all those years. Jake's approach to football wasn't about failure. It was about service.

Where can you serve? How can you learn to increase your abilities and move past your limitations? How can you begin to see that *great efforts are their own rewards*?

YOGOWYPI UNIVERSITY

Discuss a time when you put in the extra effort either for yourself or others and discuss the rewards you received from the extra effort.

List the things you feel you "have to" do, and the things you feel you "want to" do.

Is it possible to turn your "have to's" into "want to's"?

What would be different in your life if you eliminated "have to" from your perspective? How would others perceive you? What would happen to your ability to influence others if you chose to view all challenges as opportunities?

Why does the perspective of, "I have to" do something negate the effort of the put in?

Discuss the times that you strive to "get by." What does it cost you when your focus is simply on survival?

What pay-off do you get when you choose to simply get by?

What additional rewards might you receive if you chose to put 100% into everything you do?

In this chapter we discussed that "mistakes are great moments." If you choose to take an action that is destructive toward your life and others, even though you know better, is that a "great moment" or a "destructive moment"? Make the distinction and discuss the difference between the two.

Why are mistakes "great moments"?

Discuss some "great moments" you have had in your life and what you learned from them.

Feedback is the breakfast of champions! Have you ever been around someone who doesn't take feedback very well? Why do you think people are resistant to getting feedback about their previous performance?

When you make an attempt and fail what is the most useful strategy for dealing with the "great moment"? What is the most useful strategy for dealing with feedback when it comes from someone else?

The **YOGOWYPI** *Review*

Great Efforts Yield Great Rewards

The "Law of the Put In" states that if my perspective toward achieving a task is centered around "have to" then my "put in" for the task is negated.

To receive maximum value for my "put in" it is important that we act out of personal choice. If someone is "making you" do something then you get no personal credit for the "put in" and you diminish what you "get out."

We learn to be a victim based upon how we communicate with ourselves and those around us.

We live in a world filled with opportunities, and we can pretty much just show up and get by. Is getting by enough?

Mistakes are "Great Moments" if we choose to learn from our mistakes and apply that learning in the future.

Feedback is the Breakfast of Champions!

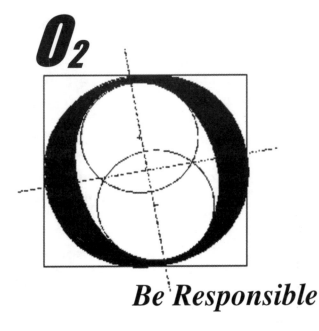

Be Responsible

Chapter 6

O2 Be Responsible

Oxygen is essential to sustain life, and no one knows that better than my son, Shannon. A few years ago, I was awakened by the sounds of my 3-year-old son gasping for life. Shannon's airway had been closed off by an infection in his epiglottis, and he was gasping for air. The only words, he managed to get out of his mouth through his labored breathing were "Help me, Dad."

I immediately picked Shannon up and rushed to the hospital as quickly as I could. When the emergency room doctor heard my son's labored breathing, he immediately called another doctor to put a tube down Shannon's throat so my son could get life-sustaining oxygen.

My son lay unconscious for the next four hours. When his condition had not improved, we made the decision to Life Watch him to a larger hospital so that he could get the care he needed to improve his condition.

It was the scariest feeling of my life knowing that my son was minutes away from not being with us, and I am thankful for the quick response of those at the hospital who helped Shannon live.

Just as oxygen is essential to life, responsibility is the necessary element to sustain healthy life choices. Without responsibility, we become burdened by the learned condition of being a victim. Sadly, most people walk around not knowing that they are choosing victimization as a pattern of behavior. Victimization limits our life choices. It pushes away those who care about us, and it destroys the quality of our life.

With responsibility, we become able to support those around us. We gain freedom we never knew we had, and we gain control over our destiny. To understand how responsibility is the essential element to make positive life choices, we must first look at some myths of responsibility.

Myth #1: Responsibility Means Being in Control

I can't control the weather. I can't control what circumstances are thrown at me, and I can't control what other people think of me. So many times, we get upset and frustrated because we try to control things that are outside of our control. We tend to want other people to act the way we want them to act, and all we do is frustrate ourselves and the people in our lives by trying to control them. When we try to control things that are outside of our influence, we are, in effect, being irresponsible.

Responsibility is about choosing to control what is in our power to control. We can choose our approach to a challenge. We can choose how to respond to a challenge. When we know the difference between what we can control and what we cannot control, we can take the responsibility for acting within our areas of influence.

Myth #2: Responsibility Comes with Age

Tom Hanks is a favorite actor of mine, and in the late 1980s, he starred in a movie named *Big.* If you have never seen this movie, add it to your list because it's a must-see movie.

In the movie, Hanks plays a character who makes a wish to be big, and his wish comes true. Overnight, he becomes a 30 year old with a 10-year-old mind.

Wanting to be big is another learned condition in our culture. We spend our youth emulating those who have gone before us, and when we reach physical maturity, we believe that since we are big, we are responsible.

The problem with this logic is that if we emulate others—even very responsible people—it doesn't mean that we're now responsible. Instead, we've merely learned how to act out the part, based on what we've seen that seems to work for others.

This is only a watered-down version of responsibility. True responsibility is a skill that requires discipline to achieve. Becoming responsible means learning to think and act in a way that enhances our ability to respond. Age has nothing to do with responsibility. Maturity does.

Myth #3: Responsibility Means Feeling Bad

Recently, a local newspaper reported about a city administrator and police officer who embezzled more than $175,000 from their city government. Upon conviction and sentencing, one of the perpetrators released a statement to the press, saying, "I feel bad for the hardworking citizens of this city and all of the people we stole from."

When I hear statements like that, I want to say, "so…now what?" I understand what people are attempting to do when they make such a statement, but taking responsibility isn't about their feelings. I realize that it's important for perpetrators to feel bad for what they've done, but there are many more steps to take in order to take full responsibility.

Feeling bad is one step. Saying sorry is another step, but I am personally more concerned about the next step. What are you going to do to make it right with us? Responsibility is much, much more than feeling bad.

Myth #4: Being Responsible Means Not Having Fun

I was walking out of my high school after basketball practice at age 15 when Barry Fisher pulled up to me and asked if I wanted a ride home. I didn't hang out with this guy because I considered him to be kind of square. I was in the party crowd, and he just didn't seem to be my type of friend. But since it was cold, I hopped in and we rode around, talked, laughed, and listened to some music.

Before dropping me off, he said that he and some of his friends were going to hang out in his basement on Saturday night watching movies. Did I want to join them? I thought for a minute and agreed. Since Barry was already aware of the company I kept, he told me, "Oh yeah, my friends and I have an agreement that when we are together, no drugs, no alcohol."

I was a little taken back by his forthrightness but, I said, "No biggie," while I wondered how this could be any fun.

That ride home was the beginning of great things for me. I had no idea at the time, but Barry's invitation wasn't just about watching movies, it was an invitation for a whole different way to live. Because of Barry, I spent the rest of my high-school years making better choices and learning how to have fun without drugs or alcohol. Barry gave me the courage to stand with him when I didn't have the courage to stand alone.

Barry is now 40 years old, and he has never touched a drug or a drop of alcohol. He has remained my best friend through all these years, and we have more fun together than anyone could imagine. We were college roommates, and now we are raising our families together. Barry lives just 50 miles away from me, and we get together every chance we get. Sometimes after a meal, when our families have been laughing so hard together that we cry, I pause and think, "What if he would not have stopped?"

Had Barry not stopped and given me a ride way back in high school, I shudder to think of the person that I might have become. Yes, maybe I missed a few parties, but what I missed, I consider a good trade. My life now is filled with joy and lots of fun.

Being responsible really means learning to gain the tools necessary to enjoy life. Too often we get caught in the trap of trying to find the quick fix. Settling for the first-available good time cuts our ability to respond to the better choices that are available.

So the next time you're needing to make a decision, remember the YOGOWYPI factor. If the choice seems like a quick and easy fix, then you're putting little effort into your solution. Instead, put a little more effort into being fun and creative, and that will lead you to a more joyous way to live.

Myth #5: Being Responsible Means I Get to Choose My Consequence

A small boy shook as his father asked him the question for the third time: "Son, did you push the outhouse into the creek?"

"No, dad it wasn't me," the son responded.

"Son, sit down and let me tell you a story. When George Washington was a boy, he took an axe to the cherry tree. When his father asked him if he had cut it down, George Washington told his dad that he could not tell a lie and that he did cut down the cherry tree. His father was so impressed with the honesty of his son, he said he would not punish his son because his son had told him the truth."

Upon finishing the story, the father once again asked his son, "Son, did you push the outhouse into the creek?"

This time the son responded in a different way. "Father, I cannot tell a lie. Yes, it was me who pushed the outhouse into the creek."

The father reached for his belt and said, "Assume the position, son, and prepare for your punishment."

Puzzled, the boy looked at his father and said, "But Dad, when George Washington told the truth, he was not punished."

The father said, "Yes, that is true son, but when the tree was chopped down, George Washington's father wasn't in it!"

So many times we believe the "George Washington theory of responsibility." We believe that if we own up to our mistakes, then we should not receive any consequences for our actions. But life doesn't work that way. We get to choose our actions in life, not our consequences.

Yet, too often, we focus more on possible consequences than on the responsible action we can take. We fail to see consequence as the great teacher. It is the consequence of our actions, and our willingness to endure the consequence that may lead to better choices in the future. Being responsible doesn't mean living without consequence; being responsible means learning to move forward with the wisdom of experience that comes from consequence.

Taking on True Responsibility

Be responsible. We have heard this phrase our whole lives. We hear teachers talk about it. Our parents give us lectures about it, and most of us think of ourselves as responsible people.

When we look closer at the word *responsibility*, we can get a clearer meaning about its intent. Responsibility is made up of two words: respond and ability. That is responsibility. It is our ability to respond to whatever life throws at us. It is our ability to make the best choice about what we know in any given situation, and it is our ability to shape our lives through the quality of our choices.

Four Thieves of Responsibility

When bad things happen to good people we have a choice. We can choose to be a victim to what happened to us or take responsibility. The four thieves of responsibility are shame, blame, deny and quit. It is these four ways of reacting to what happens to us that keeps us from taking responsibility. We could feel bad about what just happened. Feeling bad places no focus on learning in the future. If we are always feeling bad about our previous performance then our "ability to respond" goes down. We could blame others for our mistake. If we blame our boss, parents or co-workers for our mistake then we are in essence giving them power over our future. If they are responsible, then they

> *Four Thieves of Responsibility*
> 1. *Shame*
> 2. *Blame*
> 3. *Deny*
> 4. *Quit*

> *Living in freedom means I get to choose my actions; however, I don't get to choose the consequences of my actions.*

have the ability to respond, and we are waiting for them to change in order to improve our life situation. If we deny the mistake ever happened then we have no real power to make the situation better because we are not acknowledging its existence. If we quit, then we are giving up any possibility of making our life situation better.

In December of 1998, the world lost a very funny man, his name was Chris Farley, and was perhaps one of the best comics of his time. Farley had grown up watching *Saturday Night Live*, and he set his sights on being as outrageous as his role model John Belushi. Through hard work and honing his craft of making people laugh Farley eventually got a spot on Saturday Night Live and became as successful if not more successful than Belushi. Farley's fame rose and eventually, like Belushi, was asked to act in movies. Two of his movies, *Tommy Boy* and *Black Sheep* are classic comedies today.

What is interesting about Farley's life is that he modeled Belushi to a science right up until the time of his death. Good friends, and other actors tried to slow down Farley. His friend and fellow actor David Spade reportedly even told Farley, "If you don't slow down you will wind up just like Belushi." In other words, Spade worried that Farley would die at a young age, just like Belushi did.

Shortly before Farley's death, Farley was quoted in a Wisconsin newspaper as saying, "I thought there would come a day when I had enough fame, fortune, riches and popularity that the *laws of the universe* didn't apply to me anymore." He said, "I was wrong."

The Laws of the Universe

The laws of the universe apply to all of us. We can only find true joy in life when we focus on our *ability to respond* to what happens to us rather than attempting to forge our own set of laws to skirt the issue of taking responsibility. Chris Farley chose to be a victim by denying the forces of responsibility, and the toll was heavy. He died at the age of 33-the exact same age of John Belushi at the time of his death.

> *The "Laws of the Universe" apply to all of us, and true joy comes from focusing on our ability to respond to lifes' challenges.*

Denial, was the way Farley chose to victimize himself. Regardless of which one it is, shame, blame, deny, and quit are powerful forces that keep us from experiencing the richness that comes to us when we learn to focus on our ability to respond to what life hands us. Victimizing ourselves and others is the exact opposite of responsibility, and to take responsibility we must eliminate victimization from our behavior repertoire.

A Responsibility Revolution

I invite you to a totally different way of thinking and approaching life's challenges. It is revolutionary, outrageous, unique, and will vastly change and increase the amount of opportunities that are available to you in your life.

I also invite you to eliminate shame, because we can't change our past, we can only learn from it. Our past can serve us as a teacher, but has no value in determining our value as a human being.

Blaming puts you into a loop that defeats your ability to respond. It takes you out of the drivers seat, and sometimes you don't end up in the drivers seat but in the trunk. Denial, is powerful force, which is why it is important that you look at how your actions contributed to the situation you're in. Quitting is a tough pattern to break, but once the value of perseverance is learned it brings tremendous value to your life.

Relinquish-Replace the Key to Responsibility

Relinquish the behaviors of victimizing yourself. Be-gone shame, blame, deny and quit, and replace those patterns with a strategy for learning from your past so you can improve your ability to respond in the future. Replace your negative patterns with a "Sure F.I.R.E." method for empowering yourself even in the worst of circumstance.

The "Sure F.I.R.E." Technology for Responsible Results

Acquire the FIRE! Acquire the FIRE! Get passionate about relinquishing your negative irresponsible patterns and learn to use failure as a spring board to produce positive results. To relinquish your self-victimization you must follow four steps. Focus, Initiate, Respond and Experience.

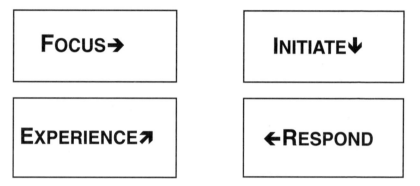

F = F.O.C.U.S. *Follow One Course Until Successful*

Choose your destiny in advance and set yourself on to a path of what's possible. What do you want to accomplish? Do you want a great career? Do you want to acquire new skill? Do you want to have an impact on the world? Do you want to be in better physical condition? Make a decision and then apply the sure-fire method by asking yourself the question. Can I live in the realm of what's possible? It all starts with *focus*. Do I have the potential? The question isn't about whether you can do it today or if you already know how to do it. The question is: Do I have the potential? Focus means to follow one course until successful. FOCUS is about looking at what's possible and living in the potential long enough to initiate an action.

I = Initiate an Action

Do something! Most people think about doing some-

thing but never do it. It doesn't matter if you don't know how to do it perfectly, just do something! Henry David Thoreau wrote "The mass of men lead lives of quiet desperation." Don't choose to live there, get out and do something that will make your life extraordinary. Initiate an Action.

I have always wanted to be an author of my own book, but never felt I had the skills to do it. I started by being a contributing author to a series of books. This process got me around writers, and I began to familiarize myself with the process. I didn't just wake up one day and say, "Today I will become an author." I first had to see it as within the realm of possibility for me.

In fact as a struggling high school and college student I could barely even embrace the notion of writing my own book. However, by spending time around other writers and speakers I started to focus on the possibility and eventually initiated an action.

Focus on what you want to achieve →

Initiate an action (do something, get involved, join a club, get out meet others, gather information)

Most people don't have a problem with step one and step two of the sure-fire method, because those two steps are about making the decision and getting started. What separates the successful from the struggling, however is step three. Instead of responding to feedback, we react. We react negatively, we victimize ourselves. We feel bad about this situation and then we remember all the other bad experiences we've had. We then stop taking responsibility because we feel so bad and we end up extinguishing our fire instead of empowering ourselves.

R = Respond vs. React

Many of us get caught into the trap that events have

meanings. Events don't have meanings we assign meaning to events based upon our belief system. We have a tendency to buy into the opinions of outside influences and use that as evidence to not initiate another action. We go out on to the basketball court of life. We shoot; we miss. Someone says, "you can't shoot baskets" and we believe them. Then we make it even harder on ourselves by telling ourselves we can't shoot baskets based upon the evidence from our past. We react instead of respond.

Experience

Mistakes are great moments. People learn to do things they didn't believe possible when they focus their attention on the experience gained rather than on feeling bad because of their failures.

By choosing to focus on what you have learned from your experience, you put yourself in a more resourceful state for overcoming the obstacles that are in front of you. This experience will empower you to initiate another action because you see yourself as a learner instead of a failure. Each action you take gives you something you didn't have before-experience. That experience increases your chances of accomplishing what you set out to do. Being responsible is not about focusing on what happened but on using what happened as a tool to make us better.

The Sure-Fire Paradigm Shift

So how does this look in real life? It depends on which path you take: the sure-fire path or the path that will end up getting you fired. Fired by who? Fired by yourself. Because you extinguish instead of experience in step 4, you end up destroying your own dream. here is what happens when you extinguish your fire, which ends up getting you fired:

> Step 1: FOCUS-I am going to be a writer
> Step 2: Initiate-I write and send it to the editor
> Step 3: React-I react to the criticism of my hard work.
> Step 4: Extinguish-I extinguish my fire.
> Step 5: Destroyed dream-I am not a writer.

Unfortunately, this is the thinking of too many people, and it leads them straight into victimization instead of responsibility. If you use the sure fire method, notice how steps three and four shift to bring you the results for which you are striving.

Step 1: Focus-I am going to be a writer.
Step 2: Initiate-I write and send it to an editor
Step 3: Respond-I respond to the feedback (even when it feels like criticism) of my hard work.
Step 4: Experience-I learn from the feedback. I integrate valid feedback and disgard what isn't.

What happens after you get to step four? Repeat steps one and two again. This time initiate a new action based upon what you have learned. Keep repeating the process until you get to where you want to go. But don't stop there. Keep reading. Developing a wisdom of mission will give you the fuel to persist and live a life that matters.

YOGOWYPI UNIVERSITY

Discuss the "myths of responsibility" and how those myths keep us from taking true responsibility.

Myths
-Responsibility means being in control.
-Responsibility comes with age.
-Responsibility means "feeling bad."
-Responsibility means not having fun.
-Responsibility means I get to choose my
   consequence.

What are the four thieves of responsiblity and how do they keep us from improving our "ability to respond" in the future?

Talk about a time when you chose either shame, blame, denial or quitting instead of focusing on your "ability to re-spond. Why did you choose that reaction instead?

Most of us have a negative dominant behavior pattern that comes up for us instead of taking responsibility. Which one is yours? Is it shame, blame, deny or quit? Why do you suppose you chose that one?

Discuss the steps of the "Sure-Fire" technology for responsible results in terms of implementing a personal change in your life. Be specific and use examples. For instance, if you decided to get all A's in your classes this semester, your "Sure -Fire" plan may look like this:

FOCUS- A focus statement about your intended result.
INITIATE-Implement a new study strategy that would move you closer to your outcome. (For example: study groups, sitting in the front of the class, using a day-planner to organize your study time etc.)
RESPOND: After the semester is over, evaluate the effectiveness of your plan. Stay out of the emotion and ask what can I do differently the next time.
EXPERIENCE: What have you learned that could improve your abilities next semester? Then, Focus, Initiate, Respond, Experience.

Write your "Sure-Fire" plan here:

The **YOGOWYPA** *Review*

Just as oxygen is essential to life, responsibility is essential to maintaining healthy life choices.

Our cultural myths about responsibility keep us from taking on true responsibility.

True responsibility focuses on our "ability to respond" to life situations.

The four thieves of responsibility are shame, blame, deny and quit.

A strategy for dealing with shame, blame, deny and quit in our lives is the "Sure-FIRE" technology for responsible results.

F-FOCUS
(Follow One Course Until Successful)
Develop an improvement plan.
I-Initiate
Initiate an action.
R-Respond
Respond rather than react .
E-Experience
Experience will support you in applying what you know about creating success.

Wisdom of Mission

Chapter 7

W = Wisdom of Mission:
Four Key Steps

Foster homes had been her life—her whole life. By the time she was 18 years old, she had lived in thirteen of them. One morning, at the age of 10, she saw a television show being broadcast live from Hawaii. In the secret recesses of her mind, she escaped to the beauty of the islands. She imagined that in a place so beautiful there couldn't possibly be problems that she encountered in her life. Her dream allowed her to endure all of the foster homes and all of the physical and emotional abuse because she knew that one day she would leave Massachusetts and move to her dream escape in Hawaii.

She told her friends of her plans, and most people just thought of her as a dreamer with no sense of mission in life. Yet getting to and living in Hawaii had become her first of many lifelong missions. In 1969, she arrived in Honolulu with two bags containing everything she owned and 50 dollars in her pocket.

It was the *wisdom of mission* that compelled my mentor, Delorese Gregoire, to take action and make her life better. However, as you may have guessed, just moving somewhere cannot make your life better. You must learn and apply solid principles to make your life work.

Delorese discovered that even in Hawaii, the most beautiful of all places, that there were problems there as well. Rather than being defeated by her discovery, Delorese enveloped the beauty of her surroundings and made it a part of her heart and journey. She allowed this beauty to captivate her mind, body, and spirit and by doing so, she created her new life mission.

Wisdom of mission is a phrase that defines what happens to us both internally and externally when we have a dream of pursuing something bigger than ourselves. When we have a dream, we can immediately have a purpose and mission in life, even though our purpose and mission are not yet defined. It is the *wisdom of mission* that allows us to define our purpose and mission so that we can take action in the direction of our dreams.

Wisdom of mission is a four-step process. First, we must have a dream that gets us excited enough to leave our O-zone. We realize that if we stay where we are, we will certainly decay, and the only out is up.

> **The Four-Step Process of the Wisdom of Mission**
>
> *Step 1: Dream*
> *Step 2: Discover*
> *Step 3: Find a Purpose*
> *Step 4: Develop a Mission*

Second, we must take action on that dream. Taking action leads us to discovery. Let's say a person has a dream of going to college and becoming a teacher. Once he becomes a teacher, he discovers that there are a lot of challenges in the teaching field. He wants to make education better, so he takes some kind of action to improve his teaching surroundings. He may work on himself to become a better teacher or work with the administration to improve the quality of education for everyone.

> **Wisdom of Mission**
> *Defines what happens to us both internally and externally when we have a dream of pursuing something bigger than ourselves.*

It is not until we are working at something that is bigger than we are that we acquire wisdom of mission. Out of this desire to make it better, we enter step three of having a purpose. But a purpose needs to be defined. By having a purpose, we enter step four: We develop a mission about the direction of our life's work.

Creating Joy

While there are many opinions about what makes a mission and how mission statements should be written, I believe one thing is clear. The essential element of a mission is it creates joy in your heart as well as in the hearts of others. When a person dreams of graduating from college, starting a company, teaching school, or becoming a doctor, all of this life work is a part of a larger-life picture. This larger-life picture, if it is a true mission, will ultimately bring joy to yourself and others.

Delorese was so captivated by Hawaii and all that she learned about herself by being there that she started two companies dedicated to bringing joy to others. Over the next 16 years of her life, Delorese founded and directed Hawaii Study Tours and Hawaii HomeStay. Both companies were committed to bringing students to Hawaii and educating them about the islands. But this was only the beginning of her mission.

As she did this work, Delorese couldn't help but notice all of the challenges that teens were having in her home

state. She discovered that the teens of Hawaii were going through the same challenges that she had faced as a teen. She found that geography can't make you happy. Being in a beautiful place can be breathtaking, and it may bring us a temporary sense of euphoria, but it can't create lifelong joy. Her life now took on a new purpose.

The True Joy in Life

*This is the true joy in life, being used for a purpose
recognized by yourself as a mighty one...
Being a force of nature instead of a feverish, selfish
little clod of ailments and grievances complaining
that the world will not devote itself to making you happy.*[1]
*I am of the opinion that my life belongs to the whole
community, and as long as I live it is my privilege
to do for it whatsoever I can.
I want to be thoroughly used up when I die,
for the harder I work the more I live.
I rejoice in life for its own sake.
Life is no brief candle to me.
It is a sort of a splendid torch,
which I have got to hold for the moment;
and I want it to burn as brightly as possible
before handing it on to future generations.*[2]

George Bernard Shaw [3]

Pursuing Your Purpose Leads to Mission

A hammer has a purpose. A hammer was created to be used. We invent new tools so that we can create new beginnings. Nothing is created without purpose. From tools to toys and from businesses to educational programs, all things have purpose.

Having purpose brings forth two challenges, and both challenges are equally important. First, we must find our purpose. Second, we must be willing to live with that purpose as a constant driving force inside of us. Finding our purpose isn't necessarily easy.

Some people have known their purpose their entire lives. When my daughter Josha came home from kindergarten on her first day, she didn't know it, but she stated her life-long purpose. "I am going to be a teacher," she said.

What Josha was really saying was, "I have found my purpose in life. I believe that I can find joy in helping others learn." Josha is a teenager now, and she has picked out her college and has held steadfast to that purpose she articulated in kindergarten. She still says she is going to be a teacher.

Delorese, even though I believe has always possessed wisdom of mission, didn't find her purpose until she was in her 30s. Colonel Sanders, the founder of KFC, didn't find his purpose of giving people joy though better tasting chicken, until his 60s. Some people find their purpose through their children and others through mentors. Some people find it by volunteering or spending time doing things they love.

Two things about finding a purpose are certain however. Before we find our purpose, we may feel uneasy or lost in the world. After we find our purpose, we feel unsettled unless we are pursuing what matters most to us.

Discovering her purpose led Delorese to put her purpose and mission into words. You can think about your purpose, but it has little power until you write it and speak it. The power of the written word will help others know if they can support you or assist you in the direction of your dreams.

Remember the SureFIRE method for expanding your O-zone. *Focus* on finding your purpose. Then *initiate* an action. After you have found your purpose, your first action is to take the time to put it into words. Writing a mission statement is the only way that you can be sure that you are following your plan. By writing your purpose in a mission statement, you can test your actions to see if you are on track.

Clarity of Purpose Brings Opportunity

Witnessing the power of a defined purpose made me an instant believer in the critical role of speaking about your purpose on a daily basis. I was speaking about my purpose that led to Delorese in the first place.

While attending an adult training, I told a large group of adults about my purpose. Immediately following the session, Pat Michaels, a fellow participant approached me and told me that a woman named Delorese Gregoire had a program for teens that her son had attended. Pat gave me Delorese's phone number, and I called Delorese about working as a staff member in her program for teens.

Synergy was now at work. By telling others about my purpose, someone saw that Delorese and I had common life missions. Pat became the intermediary who put us together. Had either one of us been unclear about our purpose, the connection would not have been made.

Some people like to get metaphysical about things like this, and they call it the universe bringing people together. I simply call it clarity. I believe that people naturally want to help, and when someone spots similarities, he or she will support you in filling your needs. Without clarity of purpose, others will not know how to help you. I met Delorese because Pat, Delorese, and I all had a clarity of purpose.

Delorese, started a program in Hawaii to support teen success. Her clarity of purpose led her to create Winners' Camp, a seven-day residential program designed to support teens of Hawaii in gaining tools for lifelong success. This is her purpose statement:

> To empower teenagers to break through limiting barriers and move towards greater success in their lives. To give teenagers the tools for accelerated learning, thus re-kindling the joy and fun of learning, as well as inspiring excellence.
>
> Winners' Camp
> Manual, 1985

Clarity of Purpose Leads to Unveiling Your Mission

Atop a hill, in Oakville, Alabama, sits a statue of Jesse Owens, the man who single handedly humbled Hitler's Aryan supremacy theory by taking home four gold medals in the 1936 Olympic Games. The statue was unveiled in July of 1996 and sits as a great tribute to a man who lived, ran, and spoke with a mission.

Through his actions, Owens taught the world that we should be measured by our actions not by the color of our skin. However, long before the statue was unveiled in Oakville, Alabama, Owens' purpose and mission existed in his heart. Long before you are given credit for your actions, your purpose and mission must be unveiled within you.

An unveiled mission statement describes your life's work. It is a statement that brings forth energy and possibility about what you are doing with your life. It already exists, just as Jesse Owens' life mission existed before the statue was created. An unveiled mission is a selfless statement that describes your purpose. The pursuit of your mission brings joy to you and the people around you, and it is bigger than a single person. An unveiled mission is usually community, region, or world based in its approach.

In addition to having a mission statement that has a clarity of purpose, Delorese also has an unveiled mission for Winners' Camp. It is:

> To provide cutting-edge leadership training for Hawaiian teens, their teachers, and their families; To awaken teens to their personal and community potential.
>
> Winners' Camp
> Manual, 1985

Since 1985, when Winners' Camp was established, Delorese and her staff have trained more than 9,000 teens and adults throughout Hawaii and beyond. Graduates from Winners' Camp have gone on to become teachers, doctors, lawyers, psychologists, scientists, and parents. Of those who have been trained, most say Winners' Camp is the agent of change that turned them around and started them thinking of achieving possibilities bigger than themselves.

Developing Your Wisdom of Mission

You can develop your wisdom of mission in many different ways. Here are a few ideas to get your started:

Don't be lolo—In Hawaiian, the word *lolo* means crazy. Many times, we shortchange ourselves because we think crazy. Lolo thinking is when we choose to limit ourselves by what I call belief attachment. We see other people achieving great things, and we think: "I could never accomplish that because I _____ (fill in the blank)." We fill our heads with crazy thoughts and then believe them because of past experience.

If we would let go of these crazy beliefs, we would quickly see that our past experience actually can create fuel to push ourselves beyond our perceived limitations. My friend Loren Lasher uses lolo as an acronym. In his programs, he says that lolo means *lock on lock out.*

When we *lock on* to the possibility that we are right about our limitations, then we *lock out* the possibility of it being different. Spend time with people who are possibility thinkers and push yourself to be open to the possibilities of what you might become.

Change your environment—Environment is critical in changing the way you think. If you find yourself feeling negative at school all the time because school is filled with negative people, then chances are you are either not living creatively enough, you are in a situation that needs to be changed, or you are hanging out with people who don't respect your purpose. If you know you're taking the right classes, maybe you need to find a different teacher—or different friends. If it's difficult to change classes, consider changing something in your study area that brings in more possibility and positivity.

Listen to your physiological cues—On any given day, your mind, body, and spirit experience a wide array of emo-

tions. Your emotions have a physiological affect on how you feel. Sometimes we experience changes in our head, face, neck, shoulders, gut, and legs. When things happen in your life, virtually every part of your body changes somehow. Take note about what makes your heart race, what makes you settle down, what causes you to be squeamish, what creates euphoria, what makes you laugh, what makes you joyful, what makes you giddy. Our body gives us cues to what we are most passionate about in our life. Cultivate this awareness and use

it as means of turning your passions into opportunities.

Go to kindergarten—A few years ago, I was asked to do a keynote address to a group of about 10,000 high school students about stopping the violence in America. For some reason, I decided that the best place to gain the wisdom was not to talk to older people but to seek out younger people. I set up a date with a local kindergarten class, and I went in to ask them some questions. It just so happened that I was speaking to this class when they were all wearing red ribbons.

"Why are you wearing red ribbons?" I asked.

"It's Red Ribbon Week," they said.

"And what is Red Ribbon Week about?" I asked.

Dustin responded, "This is the week where we celebrate drugs."

I wanted to laugh, but instead I said, "Yes. This is the week where we celebrate saying no to drugs."

I then asked if they could help me tell the big kids in America how to stop the violence in our schools. Hands went into the air without hesitation. Their answers flew through the air. Here is what they said:

"Be Nice."

"Share."

"Ask if you can help them."

"Give hugs."

"Tell them to take a time out."

"Tell them to remember if you are not nice, you won't get gummy bears."

The last boy with his hand in the air said, "If someone's car is on fire, you should give them a ride home."

As I was leaving the room. one girl said to me, "If those big kids don't know how to be nice to each other, tell them to come and see us. We already know how."

She was 100% correct. If we spend time around where we have been, we would understand how precious our life is. So spend time in your local schools. Volunteer. Attend plays, recitals, and sporting events. When we connect with our communities, we develop a sense of who we are and what is most important in our lives.

Ask yourself interesting questions—If I could have my life be anyway I wanted it, what would that look like? What if money didn't matter? What if where I lived didn't matter? What matters to me the most? What brings me the most joy? Who are the people who have had the most influence on me? What is hope? What is love? What does it mean to care? What question could I ask myself right now that would send me into deep thought?

Attend a seminar outside of your field—You often can discover lots of new ideas from other subjects, even ones that you wouldn't think have much to offer. Read a magazine outside of field of interest. Talk to people who take different classes. Find out what gets other people excited and what new possibilities you can find.

Volunteer—Get involved in community projects. Join your local chapter of Habitat for Humanity. Go on a mission for spring break instead of going to a beach. You will be amazed at the depth of friendship you will develop in a short time. Go bowling for kids' sake. Do a relay for life. Answer phones at a telethon. Work with Special Olympians.

We earn money when we work, but we learn who we are when we volunteer. Volunteering gives us a way to interact with our hearts, as well as our hands, and it opens doors to deeper friendships by teaching us how to connect with others. When we volunteer we always receive more than we give!

There are many ways to develop our wisdom of mission, and these are but a few examples. By committing yourself to new possibilities, you will naturally dream about what it would be like to work in an area where you feel you are making a contribution. That new sense of awareness will lead you to discover more about yourself, which will help your purpose and mission in life to evolve. Write down what you dream. Then take action. Focus. Initiate. Respond. Experience.

Removing the Have tos from Your Life
You can remove the have tos from your life. All you need to do is to choose. I believe there are four critical choices that can make the difference. These include: choosing to live with a smile on your face and love in your heart, choosing to be more attractive, choosing to live longer, and choosing to brighten the room on the way in.

Choose to Live with a Smile on Your Face and Love in Your Heart
My good friend Kent Boggs is the executive director for Oklahoma's Future Farmers of America (FFA). Each year, he takes on the challenge of holding summer camp for nearly 1,500 campers. During camp, participants get involved in sessions led by state officers and college-age, small-group leaders. They get involved with speakers, and they participate in numerous leadership and team-building activities. It is a great experience and perhaps one of the best leadership opportunities for young FFA members.

While working with and training his leaders, you will often hear Kent say, "Live with a smile on your face and love in your heart." I have heard him say it many times, and I know that he is not just saying it because it is a catchy phase. I have grown to understand that this is Kent's philosophy for living well.

Do we smile because we are happy or are we happy because we smile? I am not sure. But I do know that after using Kent's advice over the past several years, I feel better. I spend my days walking into America's colleges and high schools, and I have noticed an incredible difference since I have started smiling more.

I love my job, and I have always loved what I do, but since I started making a conscious effort to smile more, I have found even more joy in my work. When I walk into a school or a difficult situation I have noticed that people respond better to me when I am smiling.

Choose to Be More Attractive

A smile makes you more attractive. I mean the true meaning of attractive, not what our society defines as attractive. The true meaning of attractive is that people will be drawn toward you. A smile does that.

You may have learned about this when you were a new kid in school or when you were a rookie on the job. If you entered a room full of strangers, you probably looked around the room. Most likely, the person who smiled at you first is the one you were drawn toward.

We feel attracted to people who smile because a smile communicates safety and acceptance. Choosing to smile more can literally attract people into your world.

There are many ways to develop our wisdom of mission, and these are but a few examples. By committing yourself to new possibilities, you will naturally dream about what it would be like to work in an area where you feel you are making a contribution. That new sense of awareness will lead you to discover more about yourself, which will help your purpose and mission in life to evolve. Write down what you dream. Then take action. Focus. Initiate. Respond. Experience.

YOGOWYPI UNIVERSITY

What is your life purpose? Write a statement of your life purpose below. Use the Winners' Camp purpose statement on page 93 as a model for your own purpose statement. It should be consistent with how you see yourself making an impact on the world.

```
┌── My Purpose ─────────────────────────────┐
│                                           │
│                                           │
│                                           │
│                                           │
│                                           │
└───────────────────────────────────────────┘
```

Do you have a personal mission come to mind? If so, what is it? Write you life mission in the space provided. Use the Winners' Camp mission statement on page 94 as a model. Make sure it is action oriented and it is something that motivates you and gets you excited about your life purpose.

```
┌── My Mission ─────────────────────────────┐
│                                           │
│                                           │
│                                           │
│                                           │
│                                           │
└───────────────────────────────────────────┘
```

If the fire of your mission and purpose is not breathing inside of you already then go do the exercises on pages 95-101 until you develop a sense of how you will impact your world. When you are sure then come back and write your purpose and mission statements.

The **YOGOWYPI** *Review*

Wisdom of Mission

Wisdom of Mission describes what happens to you both externally and internally when you have a dream of persuing something bigger than yourself.

The four steps to developing your
"Wisdom of Mission" are:
1. Dream
2. Discover
3. Find a Purpose
4. Develop a mission

Pursuing your purpose will develop your mission.

Clarity of purpose will unveil your mission.

Some strategies for discovering your mission:
Don't be LOLO.
Change your environment.
Ask yourself interesting questions.
Go to kindergarten.
Listen to physiological cues.
Attend a seminar outside your field.
Volunteer.

Chapter 8

Y = Y2 LEARN:
Six Helpful
Learning Tools

Salome El of Roberts Vaux Middle School wanted his students to understand that education was a vital and important part of their lives. He had seen too many students of this inner-city Philadelphia school focus all their attention on becoming sports stars only to find themselves on the streets wishing they had received an education while they had the chance. El felt that his students were unmotivated in the classroom because the only stars in their world were connected to athletics. A former athlete himself, El had escaped the trappings of inner-city thinking and wanted his students to have a burning desire to be recognized for their intelligence.

El had seen a PBS video documentary about students who attended Roberts Vaux Middle School years ago and their tradition for excellence as chess champions. He wondered if that tradition couldn't somehow be resurrected. El knew that if they were to once again become national champions in chess, his students would have to have the desire to do so rather than be forced to do so.

> *El had escaped the trappings of inner-city thinking and wanted his students to have a burning desire to be recognized for their intelligence.*

So he and another teacher went to the cafeteria during lunch and simply started playing chess. Before long, a crowd of students gathered around the table. Some students said, "I could beat you Mr. El." Others made comments about which move he could do next. Finally a student asked, "Can I play?" These two teachers then proceeded to set up chessboards. Each day during lunch, students now spend their time playing chess.

The Energy Grew

The desire to learn the game spread throughout the school. Students soon were asking for coaching, and they wanted more time to play and learn the game. Eventually, El made himself available one hour after school each day.

El told his students when you lose, just replay the game in your mind and think about what you would do differently the next time you play. Before long, students started beating him. He and the other teachers started to notice that the students who were playing chess also were becoming more interested in school as well. He knew the stage was set to begin a formal chess program at Roberts Vaux.

In the first year, El took a few teams to play against some local schools. They did very well, and by the end of the year, he said he wanted to take a team to the national championships the next year. In a meeting with his students, he laid out the plans of how they would make their run at making it to the national championships.

Learning Tool #1: Stacking

El was successful at Roberts Vaux because he understood a simple tool called *stacking*. Intelligence is fostered in a positive environment. When individuals achieve positive success in one area of life, they will *stack* these experiences so they spill over into other areas of life. El's chess students not only succeeded in chess, they also started succeeding in school. Success breeds success, and we can't help but gain confidence in other areas in our lives when we are successful.

Learning Tool #2: Inside Out not Outside In

Filling our heads with facts and figures from a textbook  is not an education, yet many educated people have received degrees through this process. This is called outside-in education. Many of us have spent our lives sitting in classrooms getting information from the outside and trying to force it into our brains. I know because I am one of them. It wasn't until I got the burning desire to learn that I got an education.

Now as a student of life, I educate myself more every day than I ever did as a student. The difference is desire. Through stacking, El gave his students the gift of desire, which started their true education because it got them thinking. El's students were now reaching out from the inside. When we reach out because of our internal desire to learn, we get

> *When we reach out because of our internal desire to learn, we get an inside-out education.*

an inside-out education. An inside-out education is the only way we truly learn.

Learning Tool #3: Get WHYS

Getting an education is a lifelong process, and we are most effective when we have a reason for learning. Some people are motivated by external factors, such as success or money, which are goals that can take us a long way. However, true education only occurs when we have an internal passion that drives us to be more.

Learning Tool #4: Chunking and Modeling

Once El's chess players caught the desire to learn, they began chunking, which is the process of breaking things down into smaller parts. How do you eat an elephant? It only happens one bite at a time. A ten thousand mile journey begins with a single step.

Chunking is based upon the principle that we can't learn less. As you go through your life, you are

> *Chunking is the process of breaking challenging skills and tasks into smaller more manageable pieces. It is based upon the premise that we can't learn less!*

only learning more. Sometimes we focus our learning in the wrong direction, but it is impossible for you to be dumber today than you were yesterday. Since we are always gaining information, it is up to us to apply our past lessons to our future. The application of past lessons that we acquire chunk by chunk is called wisdom.

Modeling is the process of finding people who have already acquired the wisdom you desire and spending time with them. Modeling accelerates the learning process because we have a chance to learn from the mistakes and past experiences of others. When El's students started to beat him at chess, he brought in other students to learn from their strategies.

> *Modeling is finding someone who has already acquired the wisdom you desire and spending time with them.*

Many of us get into a rut because we spend much of our time around the same people day in and day out. By doing so, we limit our opportunities because we only live up to what we are exposed to on a daily basis. By expanding your circle of friends, you increase your opportunities to learn quickly and efficiently. You learn through modeling.

> **Three Parts to Modeling**
> 1. *Physiology*
> 2. *Internal Dialogue*
> 3. *Beliefs*

There are three parts to the modeling process. First, we must model the physiology of the person who processes the behavior we want to acquire. If you wanted to become a better golfer, then it would be best to spend time with Tiger Woods. Learn how he holds the club, follows through with his swing and maximizes his efforts as he makes contact with the ball. Spending time with someone who is a master at anything will increase your abilities.

Secondly, model the person's internal dialogue. Successful golfers think differently than those who golf like me. They talk to themselves differently, and when they are struggling, they have strategies for getting back in the game. By learning how successful people talk to themselves, you open yourself up to a different set of choices for improving your behavior.

Lastly, learn the person's beliefs about the activity. People who have mastered any given skill have a whole different set of beliefs from those who are average. Not only do they think differently, but their beliefs shape the way they see failure, setbacks, success, and mastery.

You might be thinking, "I don't have access to Tiger Woods." If you want to become a professional golfer, then find the best person you know and start from there. That person may not be Tiger Woods, but there are people who are Tigers all around you. Some may be Tigers because they are master chess players, mathematicians, accountants, bankers, teachers, parents or even friends. Your world is filled with people who are good at what they do.

Your job is to seek out the Tigers in your life so you can model their behaviors and become a master in all areas of your life. Become a member of an association in your area of expertise. Become an

> *Seek out the Tigers in your life so you can model their behaviors and become a master in all areas of your life.*

affiliate member of an association outside of your profession. Sit on a nonprofit, association board. Become active in your church. Get involved in city government. The key is to seek out people who are good at what they do and learn about how they developed their passion and desire so you can make their skills a part of your repertoire.

Learning Tool #5: Chunk Down then Chunk Up

When learning a new skill, mastering a behavior, or understanding a concept, chunk down then chunk up. Re-

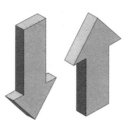

view what you have learned and then chunk up to a new level. If you are studying physics, go back to similar equations that you have mastered and re-master them. Once these equations become second nature, chunk up to a higher level.

By getting yourself to an unconscious state of competence, you will increase your ability to learn at a higher level.

El coached his students effectively by getting them to believe in what they were already good at and then encouraging them to take on tougher challenges. Sometimes that may mean taking a class more than once or going slow at first in order to go fast later (which is particularly helpful when learning a musical piece). Master basic algebra before taking advanced algebra. There is no

> *Chunk down to the last point of mastery and review then chunk up to more difficult challenges.*

shame in taking a class more than once (or auditing it the

second time around) or learning something slowly because people all learn at different rates. It is better to chunk down and master a skill at a different level than to live in a state of grief for a semester because the chunk is too large to comprehend.

Learning Tool #6: Class It Up

Education is a game, and making it a game is not intended to belittle your education experience. It is my belief that we learn best through play, and our mind is most engaged when we are playful and passionate about the subjects we are studying. Through play, we learn to question ideas, expand our knowledge base, and think about challenges in different ways. By making education a game, we engage all of our resources and increase the opportunity for an optimal learning experience.

Spend time on any college campus today and eventually you will notice the different strategies students use to approach class time. I have noticed a remarkably different approach toward going to class between the super-successful student and the one who struggles. The differences are subtle at first, but any seasoned professor can spot the dedicated from the detached in a heartbeat. If you want to succeed as a student, it is your responsibility to model the distinctions of the determined so that you become one of the dedicated rather than one of the detached.

Great students, just like great mechanics are hard to come by, but being a great student doesn't need to be a mystery. Take Steve my mechanic, for example. He is a master mechanic because he is passionate about anything with the name Toyota. He can tell you the make and model of almost every Toyota ever built, and he can tell you things about these cars that most mechanics fail to think about.

When Steve hears the engine of a Toyota running, he can tell you exactly what needs to be done to get the engine running in peak performance. Not only does he see things that most mechanics don't see, he also has the uncanny ability to explain to me what needs to happen in language that I understand. Steve, is a master mechanic who is passionate about his work, and because of his ability to catch the subtleties, he makes the invisible visible for people like me.

Seasoned students have these same kinds of abilities. They have spent time figuring out subtle distinctions about how to learn. By using the six key learning tools, they maximize what they get out of learning by what they put in.

YOGOWYPI UNIVERSITY

*Intelligence is fostered in a positive environment. By placing students in an environment in which they are nourished, El discovered that success creates more success. Discuss your educational environment and the effect it has on education.

*Discuss your internal education environment. How do you talk to yourself during the learning process? Are you your own worst enemy, or do you talk to yourself in a way that fosters your desire to learn?

*Learning happens best if the desire to learn is in place before you attempt to cram facts, figures and numbers into your head. Do you take the time to think about why you are learning what you are learning, or do you do it just because it is going to be on the test?

*Do you know why you are here, and why you are learning? What are your reasons for being here? What merits are there to learning something that you will never apply in the future? Should we study theories that we will never see again? Why or why not? What case could you make for studying a subject that will never be used in the "real world"?

How can you use the process of chunking and modeling to learn more in a short period of time?

What are the three parts to modeling and why are they useful for learning more in less time?

Who gains more in the education process the student who is very smart, gets good grades, and has to study very little or the student who struggles to makes B's and C's and has to study all the time? If you were a business owner, who would you rather hire? Why?

Class It Up is a learning model that will be covered extensively in chapter 9. In this model we will study the habits of successful students. What do successful students do that struggling students do not do? Be specific in your answer.

Y2 Learn - Six Helpful Learning Tools

With an internal desire to learn the following six principles increase in effectiveness geometrically:

1. Stacking
The process of stacking positive experiences on top on one another

2. Inside Out not Outside In Education
Gaining the internal desire to learn

3. Get WHYS
Knowing why you are doing what you are doing

4. Chunking and Modeling
The process of breaking learning down, and doing what the masters do

5. Chunk Down-Chunk Up
Going back to the last point of mastery, then increasing the intensity

6. Class It Up
The strategy that will be covered in detail in Chapter 9.

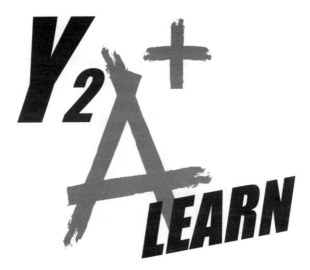

Chapter 9

Y = Y2 LEARN:
Six Character Traits
of Successful
Students

How do you maximize your classroom time so you can do more with the same amount of effort? By using the six character traits of successful students. These traits helped me move from D's and C's to A's and B's, and it has helped thousands of students across the country. It is so simple yet so profound that you will wonder how you ever got along without it. In short, these are the rules for playing and winning the education game.

The class-it-up method show the six essential character traits for playing the education game:

1. C = Communicate confidence.
2. L = Lean forward; physiology is everything.
3. A = Ask questions constantly.
4. S = Speak positively to yourself.
5. S = Sit up front in the t–zone.
6. Class it up by getting to know your professors.

1. C = Communicate Confidence

Whether you realize it or not, instructors are constantly looking and evaluating your non-verbal cues. The best professors do this because they are checking in to get feedback about the quality of their message. They take time to evaluate and notice students' reactions, and they also make decisions about your abilities as a student.

That's why it's essential to use good communication skills. I call this the non-verbal advantage. This will not register with every professor or instructor, but it will with some. Remember, to boost your GPA you don't have to get every professor to notice your diligence, only a few.

The harder you try not to participate and not to communicate with your instructor, the louder your message becomes. If you walk into class, and make a decision to be aloof, lay low, and not

> *To boost your GPA you don't need to get every professor to notice your diligence, only a few.*

get involved, you are screaming the following message to

the front of the room: "Just leave me alone. Give me my grade because all I want to do is survive this class and move on to the next one." This is not a good message to give to the person who has power over your destiny in the classroom.

Unfortunately, I learned the aloof lesson the hard way. In my early college years, I chose to act cool during class and was non-committal in my approach. Acting cool has certain physiological characteristics, and professors can read it like a worn-out novel. This physiology of treating the classroom as your living room where you act like you are watching late-night TV may be

> *Really cool students usually wind up in not-so-cool dead-end jobs because they received not-so-cool grades.*

comfortable, but it will be costly. Really cool students usually wind up in not-so-cool, dead-end jobs because they received not-so-cool grades. So if you want a strategy to get you into a dead-end job as fast as possible, just sit back, relax, be aloof, and you will get there much faster.

The benefit-of-the-doubt syndrome—Let's face it, what you are really working for is the benefit of the doubt. Communicating that you don't care doesn't work in your favor when grade time comes around. Put yourself in your professor's situation. If you have a student who is borderline between a B and a C, and during your class, this student has been as much fun to teach as a lump of lead, what are you going to do? You will probably give that student a C. The student doesn't seem to care anyway, so what difference does it make?

Contrast that with the student who shows up for class on time, participates in class, is fun to be around, and seems to have an interest in the subject you are teaching. What would you do? Some professors might just give that student the benefit of the doubt and bump that student up to a B. Some will; some won't, and if they don't, what have you lost? Nothing! You have just maximized the education for which you paid.

Remember: some professors will reward you. If 10 professors reward you for your participation, how will that affect your GPA? Some students even think that their class is too large and the professor will never notice them. Even in large classes, professors get to know a few students, and you want to make sure you are one of those students.

> *If 10 professors give you the benefit of the doubt how will that affect your GPA?*

Build your network—You may have large classes as a freshman, but you may see that professor again as an upperclassman. That professor may be

teaching an upper division smaller class later on, and if he or she remembers you as the diligent, hard-working student from a few years ago, your foot is already in the door for the possibility of getting the benefit of the doubt later in your college career. That professor may support you with a challenge later, and he or she may even want to sit on your master's thesis committee.

Instructors have lots of power in the student world, and it is important that you learn the skills for building bridges and networks so you can reap the rewards. You never know when you may cross paths with an instructor again, so make every effort to create quality interaction with every professor you meet. From the first moment you walk into a classroom to the last day of class, establish yourself as a confident student who is going someplace. If you act that way, then professors will treat you that way. You are the business of You Incorporated, a business that will one day earn money, make even more contributions, and have a network of people to rely upon.

Communicating confidence is an approach issue— When you first enter the classroom at the beginning of a semester, establish yourself as a confident student. To be confident means to carry yourself as mature, responsible, and ready. Your appearance should communicate more than you just barely got out of bed to make it to class. If you are boastful or overbearing, your efforts will work against you.

Be confident. Take interest from the beginning. Be supportive of the professor. Show respect and never try to intimidate or be threatening to your professor. If you need to confront a specific issue, make an effort to do it one on one. No good can come from embarrassing a professor in front of his or her students. Sometimes we may feel intimidated or overwhelmed by a professor or a new environment. This is normal, but be aware that sometimes a sober, non-emotional demeanor can often be miscommunicated as judgmental or uncaring. Go to class with a smile on your face and love in your heart and bring an attitude of eagerness and willingness to learn into the class-room even if you don't feel like it. The simple truth is astounding. Subtle, supportive confidence is perceived as intelligence. Become your own self-ful-filling prophecy.

Pay attention to *how* you sit in the classroom, and be aware of what message you are sending to the front of the room. Sit up straight with confidence.

> *Subtle, supportive confidence is perceived as intelligence.*

Breathe easily. Confidently tell yourself that you are pre-pared. Make eye contact with the professor and work to make the experience fun, no matter how difficult that might be at the moment.

2. L = Lean Forward; Physiology Is Everything

Communicating confidence is something you do to build relationship in the classroom. Leaning forward is something you do for yourself to keep your head in the game. Physiology is the positioning of your body, and how you position your body determines how you feel on a moment-to-moment basis.

If you were to ask 100 people to sit the way they would sit if they were tired and depressed, you would find amazing striking similarities to each person's physiology. They would slump, drop their shoulders, drop their eyes and head, retreat inward, breathe in a shallow manner and probably think, "I am so tired and depressed." If you ever want to get tired and depressed, this is an excellent strategy. This is exactly what your mind

"LEAN FORWARD."
State Management Tools for the Classroom

State management is the ability to create the state of mind you want by changing how you use your body. When you use these state management tools, you take responsibility for your educational experience. Instead of having the state choose you, you choose the most appropriate state for maximizing your education.

16 great state management tips:

1. Sit up straight.
2. Lean forward.
3. Breathe deeply.
4. Run your brain.
5. Open your eyes.
6. Increase the speed of your internal dialogue.
7. Vary the pitch in which your professor speaks.
8. Vary the tonality in which your instructor speaks.
9. See your professor acting out the part.
10. Look for ways to discover.
11. Discover why others have passion for the subject.
12. Look for humor.
13. Put a smile on your face.
14. Be grateful for your opportunity to learn.
15. Tell yourself, "I am joyful, alive, and passionate."
16. Seek out opportunities to participate.

and body do when depression sets in.

To keep your head in the game, put your body in the game. Sit the way you would sit if you were the most passionate, energetic, alive person in the world. If you asked 100 people to do this, they would sit up with their back straight and lean slightly forward with anticipation. Their breathing would deepen, and their pulse would increase. Their eyes would open wide, and internally they would probably think, "I feel good. I am ready!"

The mind-body connection—The bottom line is that we have an incredible capacity to increase the rate at which  we learn if we use the mind-body connection to our advantage. Most people already do this, but they do it negatively. They convince themselves that they are about to take part in the most boring adventure of all times, and they slump, think depressing thoughts, and get bored. *Boring people get bored.*

Interesting people have the capacity to make anything exciting. They ask questions. They look for connections and increase their interest. They sit in the wonder of discovery about the passions of others.

You are being educated when you move past the realm of boredom into the realm of discovery. It is at this point, that your education begins. Hey, if you can make time with your friends exciting, think of your capacity to make education exciting!

Create the state of mind you desire by changing your physiology for getting the job done. Put your body in motion, and your mind will follow. It takes some practice at first, but once you get good at it, you can almost dare your instructors to bore you, and they will never succeed. This is what great athletes do before they compete. They have strategies for getting their mind and body into optimal performing states. Great musicians have a pre-performance routine they each go through to get themselves in the right state to have a great performance. Actors go through a series of routines to insure that they are playing the part with truth, richness, and authentically. As students, we need to do the same thing. We need to prepare our mind and body so we can be peak performers in the classroom

Strategies for eternal, internal interest—On some occasions, you may not be interested in the subject you are learning, and it seems that no matter what you  do, you just can't seem to get yourself involved. At this point, realize that you have infinite creativity in your brain and that humans have an endless capacity for listening creatively. Oftentimes, I hear students complain, "I try to stay alert, but the instructor speaks in such a monotone voice that I can't stand it." That happens, but successful students still get through and succeed. How? By knowing that the voice inside their head runs at an almost constant 600 words per minute when they are engaged. The average instructor speaks at less than 200 words per minute. This leaves an incredible gap of nearly 66% of time where you can be recreating the lecture.

> *We have an infinite capacity for listening creatively.*

Use this time to animate, repeat, put it into characters, speed up, slow down, emphasize or restructure the lecture so that you will comprehend the lecture. If you are taking notes, you still have time to rework and reinvent the lecture as it is being delivered. It takes an extreme amount of focus to rework a lecture as it is being delivered, but over time, you will become quite proficient at it. Then you will discover that your comprehension level will increase, thus decreasing the need to take such meticulous notes.

Be playful with the lecture—As you take notes in class, place emphasis on different words. Put the lecture to the music of your choice. Make up chants. Imagine the lecture as a cheer or a chant. Make your instructor do back flips as he or she makes certain points of emphasis. Imagine your professor as Tom Cruise, Jennifer Aniston, or Samuel Jackson. How would Darth Vader deliver Newton's Law of Motion? Create grand gestures. Put them in costume.

None of this is meant to be disrespectful; it is merely a strategy to increase your ability to comprehend. After class, review your notes and write additional notes about what you were doing with the lecture in your mind when the instructor was making those points. You will discover that come test time, you have created a series of anchors that will allow you to recall the information.

Warning: Sharing your creative thoughts, characters, and ideas will make you look pretty weird, but it will increase your comprehension. This is not intended to dishonor an instructor; it is merely a tool to increase your ability to learn effectively.

3. A = Ask Questions

Asking questions is a skill, and like any skill, it takes practice. In the college classroom, we ask questions for

two reasons. The first is to involve ourselves in the lecture. The second is to get information. When we involve ourselves in the lecture, we bring forth productive mental states that enable our ability to learn. It also communicates to the instructor that you care, which increases your ability to receive the benefit of the doubt.

We can ask questions both internally and externally. When we are in the learning state, our mind should be filled with questions. Why did the professor state it that way? What is the meaning of his or her emphasis on that point? Why is the professor so passionate about this portion of the lecture? These internal questions can help you notice key points of the lecture.

> *When we involve ourselves in the lecture we bring forth productive mental states that enable our ability to learn.*

Make it a point to ask an external question every lecture. By looking for the question, you will be following each point made. This also ensures that you are keeping pace with the content. Some lessons learned through developing the skill of questioning.

• Asking questions is a skill. Just because we know what a question is doesn't mean we have the ability to ask questions. We must constantly cultivate this skill by staying in the question.

• People love to talk about things they know about. If you learn to ask the right questions, you will learn to open their vault of information. Practice getting people into interesting conversations by asking productive, inquisitive questions.

• When you take interest in others, they will like you and do just about anything to support you.

• The world is a series of challenges to be solved, and our ability to solve those challenges lies in our ability to formulate and ask the right questions.

• What you already know is not nearly as important as having the ability to find the resources to discover what you need to know.

• Asking questions communicates that you care.

Developing the skill of questioning—Do you know the best place to master the skill of asking questions? Is it possible that it is an environment in which you are already familiar? Is it also possible that you could be missing one of life's most valuable lessons even though it is right in front of you?

Have you figured out the answer? Do you still need more time? What kind of clues do you need? What do you think? Is it possible to write an entire paragraph using only questions? Do you know where you can develop the skill? Is the answer all around you?

Your educational environment is your training ground. I'm sure you figured out the answer a long time ago, but the questions and the answers were all around you. You have been given the greatest training ground for developing the skill of learning to ask questions. Every day you are exposed to new ideas, new people, new cultures, and so many of us miss the opportunity. Many people go through their education thinking college is about getting the degree.

Content is only part of the reason we get an education. The rest of our education is skill based. The purpose of getting an education is not just to learn the answers, but it is to develop the skill to ask good questions. Questioning is a skill. If you are not using your education as an opportunity to sharpen these skills, then you are missing the whole point of education.

Practice leads to mastery—When we master the skill of questioning, we open up a variety of opportunities. If you have a question, chances are someone else has the same question as well. However, when you ask the question, you receive the following benefits:

1. You gain the skill of articulating and communicating a question, a skill you will be using your whole life.
2. You will listen better because your professor will be talking directly to you.
3. You will send a valuable message to the professor that you are thinking and you are interested.
4. You are taking responsibility for the rate at which you are learning.
5. You are maximizing your educational experience you paid to receive.
6. You will stay more focused.
7. You are supporting yourself in getting past one of America's #1 fears: Speaking in public.

When we ask questions, we get so much more than simply the answer to the question. You gain life-long skills that you will keep with you long after you forgotten the content taught in the classroom.

A powerful technique for asking good questions is R.E.A.C.H. When you reach for good questions, you will be handed much in return.

Respect—Always approach questions from a curiosity instead of an accusatory approach. How you ask a question is just as important as what you ask. Always thank your professors for taking the time to answer your question.

Expect and Expand—Expect that others have the same question that you do. Regardless of the answer, remember you have grown because you have expanded your O-zone.

Articulate—Practice the question several times internally before you ask so that you can articulate the question well.

Chunk down then clarify—If you are unclear about the content being taught, then chunk down your questions into small portions. As soon as you understand, then clarify what you have figured out by stating your understanding of the material back to the professor. For example, say something like, "Oh, I get it. Then X represents the quantity of an unknown number."

Help after class—If you are very unclear, don't take up too much of your peers valuable class time. Place an H in your notes and circle the H at the place where you got confused. Then get additional clarification from an instructor, tutor, peer, or graduate assistant after class.

4. S = Speak Positively to Yourself

Learning is a self-acknowledgement process. In order to learn something new, we must first give ourselves credit for something that we have learned in the past. Struggling students walk into class thinking that it will be tough and that they will get lost. Successful students spend time focusing on the content they learned in the past and then open themselves up for the opportunities to learn in the future.

We feel encouraged to work harder when someone else tells us we did a great job. We must do the same for ourselves. Each time you learn a new chunk of information, give yourself some credit and tell yourself you did a great job.

Mastering your positive and negative internal dialogue is a huge part of the learning puzzle. It's essential to constantly communicate to ourselves in positive ways so that we don't shut down the process of learning. Learning happens best in a powerful,

> *Each time you learn a new chunk of information give yourself some credit.*

positive environment. Notice when you are cutting yourself down. All of the energy we use to belittle ourselves wastes energy that could be used on learning.

Great coaches know how internal dialogue affects performance. If players are constantly beating themselves up over past mistakes, then they can't possibly focus on how they can improve. Make it a point to constantly be aware of how you are communicating to yourself while learning.

5. S = Sit Up Front in the T-Zone

This is the most significant classroom learning tool. Numerous studies have shown a direct correlation between where a student sits in the classroom and his or her ability to get better grades. The best place to sit  is in the T-Zone: the front rows and the center rows. The closer you are to front and center, the better your chance of learning quickly and easily. So much happens up front. Sitting in the T-Zone improves your ability to gain the subtle messages necessary to learn effectively. This is what you get by sitting in the T-Zone:

Facial expressions—You see subtle distinctions in your instructor's facial communication that allows you to discover what is important and what is not. Facial expressions are cues about what is important come test time. Learning how and when your instructor emphasizes certain points will save you hours of study time because you will know what to study and when to study. When you study an instructor's facial cues, you will be clued in on the most vital and important pieces of information.

The message about your seriousness—When you have a choice about where to sit, then where you sit says the most about you. Your choice says something about your attitude toward education. There is almost always room up front in the T-Zone of the classroom. Making a point about sitting in the T-Zone sends a clear and purposeful message to your instructor about your desire to do well in the class. If you want your instructors to take you seriously, make sure they know who you are by sitting in the T-Zone.

A network of people who care—When you sit in the T-Zone, you can build your network with those who are serious about maximizing their educational opportunities. Who do you want in your study group? I want people who can help me; I want the serious student. The serious students sit in the T-Zone. By sitting near them, you open up the opportunity for building a relationship with someone who is interested in getting the most out of class. They will become a resource you can rely on.

6. Class It Up by Getting to Know Your Professors

Make it a habit to get to know your professors. By developing a relationship with them, you can learn to understand what is important and what is not. Whether you are in a large or small classroom setting, the professor will get to know only a few students by name. If they know who you are, then you will increase your chances of learning and for getting a break.

Students who get to know their instructors are the students who have the ability to work with their employers, clients, and peers when they go out into the work world. If you make it a habit to build a relationship with everyone, you will develop the necessary skills to network with others.

Get to know your instructor even if you don't like him or her. Often times, we gravitate only toward people that we like or know. That doesn't help at grading time. If for some reason you clash with an instructor, then chances are that he or she sees the world differently from you. The best place to hone the skill of working with someone who is different from you is with that teacher. If you can learn how to deal with that challenge while you're still in school, you will reap many personal and financial benefits later in life.

During my last summer of college, I was motivated to do well in class because I had to earn my degree before the end of the summer or I would not be able to get my teaching job back the next year. I was teaching in a program called limited-term teaching, and it required that in my second year of teaching, that I must complete my degree.

I returned to my university thinking I had to complete 13 hours for my degree, but because I had taken so many hours at a different university, I was required to have 24 of my last 30 hours at this institution. That meant in order to complete my degree, I would have to take 24 hours, an entire years worth of course work within one summer.

I decided to apply the YOGOWYPI factor and get my degree by the end of summer. I also set a goal to complete the 24 hours and get all A's. This was a huge challenge because up until this point, the A's on my transcript totaled five, and most of those where in physical education classes.

This goal was a huge stretch for me.

One course ended before all the others, and despite my hard work, I received a B. So I renegotiated my goal to receiving 7 A's and one B for my summer term. By the end of my summer, I had 6 A's sewn up. In the other class, I was averaging a C. But I hoped to receive the benefit of the doubt from this instructor and get a B. Six A's and 2 B's would be a huge victory for me.

Educational Psychology was the class where I was averaging a C. On my first day, there was a buzz about how tough this instructor was. He was known as the instructor who weeds out the educational majors. One student, who sat in back, said that this was his third time taking the class. Someone else mentioned that this instructor's tests were tough, and he was not flexible in his viewpoint. In other words, what you got is what you got.

Dr. Daily lived up to his reputation throughout that summer. His tests were tough. (I was averaging C's.) His lectures were long, and he had a no-nonsense approach to education and his lectures. He had been teaching this class for about 30 years, and nearly every education major I knew from this institution had some type of horror story about how tough it was to get through Ed Psych.

I had heard it all before I had ever stepped into this class. I was prepared to *class it up* and see if my class-it-

up method was right. I communicated confidence. I leaned forward during the lectures. I asked questions every chance I got. I spoke positively to myself about what I understood and sought clarification when I didn't. I sat up front in the T-Zone, and I talked to Dr. Daily every chance I got. Sometimes I would see him having coffee in the student union. I would sit with him, ask questions, and tell him stories about my first year as a teacher. In short, I got to know him very well, and he was well aware of my passion to become a good teacher.

After I had taken the final exam, I was in the library when Dr. Daily's graduate assistant approached me and asked if I had seen my final grade for the class. I said I had not. She told me that the grades were posted and I should go and look.

I ran across campus to the third floor of the education building. All along the way, I as happily chanting, "I got the B. I got the B." As I went to the bulletin board, I ran my index finger down the page looking for my social security number. I found it, and I traced along the line to see an A. An A? I retraced to double check. It was an A.

I had got an A. I had gotten an A from the toughest teacher in the education department, from the no-nonsense guy who never gives a break. There were two As on the list for Educational Psychology in the summer of 1989, and one of them was from a guy who averaged Cs on his tests.

Later that day, I spoke to Dr. Daily's grad assistant and asked why I had gotten an A when I had averaged C's on the tests. She said, "Dr. Daily said that in all his years of teaching, he had never seen a student so passionate about teaching as you. He wanted to make sure that he encouraged your efforts."

A lot of people may call what I did brown nosing. Call it whatever you want, but it works! More importantly, I built my relationship that summer and met a professor who has since had a huge impact on me. With my old attitude, I would have never taken the time to get to know someone so different from me,

> *Communicate Confidence*
> *Lean Forward*
> *Ask Questions*
> *Speak Positively*
> *Sit Up Front in the T-Zone*
> *Class it Up with your Professor*

but now I understand him. When I went back to work on my master's degree, it was Dr. Daily who dropped everything he was doing to help me understand my statistical research and encouraged me to do a good job with my thesis.

By using *class it up*, I learned about Educational Psychology, but more importantly, I built a relationship and learned some valuable lessons about building a network.

Class-it-up is a tool and like any tool it is useless unless you use it. Chances are if you are a serious student you already use some of these strategies. Now is the time to apply all of the principles and gain more out of your education than just a grade. Apply these strategies, communicate confidence in the classroom, lean forward and use your physiology to your advantage, use the R.E.A.C.H technique for asking questions, speak positively to yourself, sit up front in the T-zone and you will *class-it-up!*

YOGOWYPI UNIVERSITY

Discuss the 6 character traits of successful students (C.L.A.S.S. it UP) Of these traits which do you think would have the most impact on your success as a student?

What message do you send to your professors by where you sit in the classroom? Do you believe it makes a difference? Why or why not?

Which of the six character traits do you currently use? Why do you use that particular strategy?

Non-traditional students (that is students who are not 18-21 when entering college) have a tendency to use the six character traits. Why do you think they are more likely to use these strategies? What are some things we can learn from non-traditional students?

Discuss this statement...Boring people get bored. Is this true? Why or why not?

How much of a role does your relationship with the professor play into your success as a student? Other than a good grade what are some additional benefits that can come from learning to work with and understand your professors?

The **YOGOWYPA** *Review*

Six Character Traits of Successful Students

1. Communicate Confidence
-Understand the benefit-of-the-doubt syndrome.
-Be aware of the messages you send.
-Build your network when in class.
-It is your approach that makes the difference.

2. Lean Forward
-Physiology is everything.
-Know the mind-body connection.
-Get the strategies for eternal-internal interest.
-Be playful with the lecture.

3. Ask Questions
-Asking questions is a skill that takes practice.
-Use the R.E.A.C.H. questioning strategy.

4. Speak Positively to Yourself
-Be aware of your internal dialogue while learning.
-Develop strategies for building your confidence.

5. Sit Up Front in the T-Zone
-When you have a choice about where to sit then where you sit says the most about you.

6. Class It Up by Getting to Know your Professors
-Build your network by getting to know your professors even the ones with whom you don't have a lot in common.

Chapter 10
P = People Are People-People by Design

People. People. People! We were designed to be people-people. It is the people in our lives who bring out the very best and the very worst in us. This book is a collection of stories about the people in my life who have taught me my most valuable life lessons. Without their stories, I could not tell my story. If there is one thing that is certain to me, it is that the single most important factor in determining our personal success lies in the quality of our personal relationships.

Who are the people in your life who have had the greatest impact on you? In addition to thinking about the importance of these people, uncover their stories. By doing so, you will add new chapters to your life by learning to honor and understand the people you meet and learn from each day.

Why Me?

In the story *Cipher in the Snow,* Cliff Evans, a high school student, walked off the bus, fell down face flat in the snow, and died. His former teacher, Jean Mizer, was called into the principal's office and was informed that she should tell the parents about this tragedy.

"Why me?" she asked.

"In his sophomore chronicle, he listed you as his favorite teacher."

"Cliff Evans," she said as she thought about who he was. "A quiet boy who sat in my class and never said a word to anyone. He barely spoke to me, yet he listed me as his favorite teacher."

Mizer proceeded to Cliff's house to break the news to his parents. The mother was distraught. The stepfather said the boy was too dumb to say he was sick, and then he proceeded on with his day as if nothing had happened.

Mizer went back to school and started going through Cliff's records to learn more about him. The bare sheets spoke volumes about the boy: Cliff Evans, white, never legally adopted by his stepfather, five young brothers and half sisters. The teachers who wrote comments in his record seemed to tell a story that no one had noticed. His first-grade and second-grade teachers wrote, "Sweet, shy child," and "timid but eager."

Third grade is when everything changed. The third-grade teacher had written, "Cliff won't talk. Uncooperative. Slow learner." These same comments continued though each grade.

In high school, Cliff's I.Q. was listed at 83. In third grade, it had been listed at 106. His I.Q. didn't fall below 100 until the seventh grade. Even shy, timid, sweet children have resilience. It takes time to break them.

The doctor had listed heart failure as cause of Cliff's death, but the real cause of his death was the lack of acknowledgment. How many times do we need to be told that we are nothing before we start to believe it? How many times do we get picked last and made fun of before the message starts to sink in? Cliff's whole world had treated him as if he didn't exist, and their prophecy of him had become true.

We are people-people! We have a need to communicate and interact with others, and without it we become nothing. Cliff Evans teaches us about how important it is that we interact with others. As humans we have certain needs. We need to eat. We need to sleep. We need to drink water, and we need to commune with others. It is a part of us, and we will do almost anything to be known, noticed, and acknowledged by others. Without that vital acknowledgement, we will cease to exist.

The life of Cliff Evans is an extreme example of what happens when we don't feel a connection with others. Sometimes our communal death is not physical but it becomes emotional. Sometimes we don't get the interaction we need from others, and it becomes easier to build emotional walls between us because we have been hurt. This process of shutting down emotionally from others is called *objectification*.

When We Can't Rely, We Objectify

Our need to find acceptance is so strong that our society has found ways to capitalize on these notions. Our media fills our heads with images of people who are finding acceptance through looking a certain way, and we believe that if we look like they do, then we will find the acceptance that they have found.

People are not images, and it is impossible to create a snapshot that can explain the complexity of human existence. If we can't find acceptance through positive interaction, we will seek it out in other ways. Since we are people-people, we have a need to interact and commune with other human beings. This need is so great that we will do whatever it takes to fill the void. When we can't fill the void, we will seek alternate strategies for filling the void within us. Cliff Evans could not fill the void, and sadly he died. The question becomes, "What will we do short of dying to fill the void not fulfilled by quality human interaction?"

According to Daniel Schaffer in his book, *Dancing with a Shadow*, the Eskimos devised a way of killing wolves called Tonka, which is the strategy of burying razor-sharp knives in the snow and covering them with fresh blood. When wolves would find the frozen blood, they would start licking the blood in the snow until their tongues became numb. Eventually they reached the knives, which would slice their tongue open. Since their tongues were already numb, they kept licking until they bled to death. They died not realizing that they were satisfying their desire with their own blood.

Human existence can be much the same. We all want to interact and be acknowledged by others. Sometimes we attempt to fill the voids of our lives through unhealthy strategies. We know our choices are bad, but like the wolves, we become numb to what we know because we believe we are satisfying a need. Our personal tonka might be anger, drugs, alcohol, withdrawing, shopping, conflict, food, bulimia, anorexia, sex, tobacco, or even unhealthy relationships. All of these behaviors stem from our belief that we can satisfy our internal needs through external things. Eventually, our own negative behaviors separate us from the people we love, and we die in our own blood of negative behaviors.

What is your
tonka?

Opposite of Objectification

The opposite of objectification is understanding that we  are people and that we gain self-respect by treating ourselves and others with respect. It is the YOGOWYPI principle through and through. We can't expect quality relationships if we are not being the demonstration of respect both internally and externally. If we keep putting negativity out into the world, then negativity keeps coming back to us. If we strive to put positive out into the world, then that is what comes back.

Following his lecture, Karl Menninger was asked, "What would you suggest that someone do who is deeply depressed and seems as if he or she has no direction and may even be contemplating suicide?"

"I would tell that person to go to the other side of the tracks and find people who are in need of assistance and serve them by supporting them in putting their life back together," he replied.

By respecting ourselves and going out to help out someone else, we will find the tools we need to get our lives on the right track. Life becomes an interesting circle. In exchange of giving someone what he or she needs, we get back what we need.

The Circle of YOGOWYPI

YOGOWYPI has come full circle for me many times in my life, and most cases I have gotten more back than what I have put in because I have had the benefit of many people in my network who will not settle for second best from me. The YOGOWYPI principle rings the most truth in the terms of relationships, and the following from the book *Ano Ano: The Seed* reflects this sentiment:

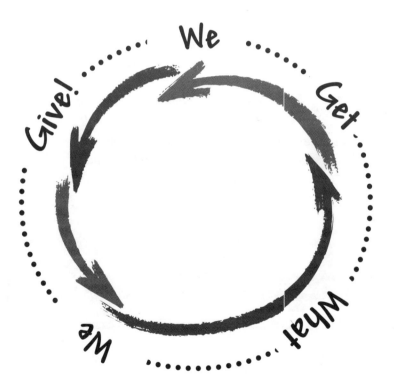

And they were taught the laws of life...
that their treatment of others
would return at last upon themselves.
Those who cheat will be cheated.
Those who slander will be slandered.
For every lie you tell...you will be lied to.
We get what we give and to the same degree.
And not always from the same
people with whom we've dealt.
But somewhere...sometime...someone
will treat you in like manner.
The good that we do to others will return also.
For your kindness to strangers you will
receive hospitatlity in far places yourself.
Understand the troubles of others who come to you
with thier souls bared...and when you cry yourself,
you will be sympathetically understood.
We get what we give.
Like always attracts like.
This is the law and it is inevitable
We cannot escape the results of our actions.
                              Kristin Zambucka

We Get What We Give

We get what we give is YOGOWYPI to the core. To deal with others, we must first understand that the world will respond to us in the way we respond to the world. Sometimes people get a little uneasy about this. Is it really true? Does the world really work like this?

I believe it does. You have heard this echoed before in different ways. Some people say: "What goes around comes around." The Bible says; "As you sow, so shall you reap." We have all heard it, but we need to live our daily lives as if it were true.

Examine this illustration and take careful note about what you see.

Most people see a picture of two islands in the ocean. Now turn the page and see if your perspective hasn't slightly changed.

Looking beneath the surface of the water we see a different perspective. There was really one mass all along. We just couldn't see below the surface. I believe the human experience is much the same, and we are all connected and dependent upon each other. When we understand the connectedness of the human experience, we also understand that I cannot hurt another without directly and literally hurting myself. Also when we support others, we will get that back as well. The key statement in Kristin Zambucka's poem is: *and not always from the same people with whom we've dealt.*

People understand the notion that if I treat you well then you will treat me well. That's a no brainer. It is the notion that somehow the world is keeping score of your actions, and your treatment of others is being returned upon you. But the world is not keeping track, you are. Whether you're doing it consciously or subconsciously, you're keeping track of your actions.

I believe that most people are morally structured. We all have a set of standards of what is right and what is wrong, and we know in our hearts whether or not we are living up to those standards. It is the consistency of our actions that attracts either positive or negative into our lives. I believe it is that consciousness that attracts opportunities that are positive and fulfilling. This is a true principle that shapes all of our interactions with other human beings.

YOGOWYPI UNIVERSITY

Are there some people in your life who seem to get better treatment than others? If so, why do you think that? Have you ever treated someone like he or she didn't matter to you simply because that person gave off the wrong impression?

Our culture uses objectification to sell products on a regular basis. Think of how the media uses "sex appeal" to sell products. What affect do you think this has on us? What about pornography and its use in our culture? What affect does that have on how we treat each other?

In the tonka example we learned that wolves will kill themselves while trying to get the blood they thirst. How does this apply to us as humans? What is your tonka? Can you give some examples of how someone went out of their way to get something even though it was killing them or thier relationships in the process?

Do you agree with the Ano Ano poem from page 151? Is it true? Discuss why you believe this to be a true principle or how you believe that it doesn't really make any difference.

Discuss the YOGOWYPI Principle and how it applies to us when we give to others. If we are giving of ourselves, do we have to give something up? Is there such a thing as unconditional giving? Have you ever given unconditionally?

The YOGOWYPA Review

We have a need to interact and communicate with others. We are all wired to be people-people, and without the connection to others we will cease to exist.

When we can't get what we want positively, we will go out of our way to get the interaction we need even though it may have a negative affect on us.

Objectification is the process of dehumanizing people and treating them as if they were objects.

The opposite of objectification is to treat others with respect.

When we respect others, that is what comes back. Keep in mind that your return may not come from the same people.

We get what we give!

Chapter 11
P = People-People Understand Communication

Our lives are filled with challenges, conflict, and sometimes problems. Most of the opposition we experience in life comes to us because of challenges in communication. Businesses fail when they don't meticulously attend to communication. Poor communication costs us billions of dollars a year in raised taxes and missed revenues. It can lead to hostility, apathy, and even war.

Communication is the single most important conduit that allows you to reach your world. Master communication, and you will move the masses. Overlook its importance, and you will be moved by the masses and into the despair of the downtrodden and defeated.

Communication Is Two Way

Communication is a two-way, continuous, irreversible, dynamic process. That's your standard, textbook definition of communication. While this definition is true, it does little to express how understanding how communication can transform life.

During my live seminars, I ask participants who is the sender and who is the receiver. Usually someone says that I am the sender, and they are the receivers. I then ask if any of them have stood in front of a group before. Those who have know that a group sends as many messages to a speaker as the speaker sends to the group. Communication is always two way. We are constantly sending and receiving messages.

Communication Is
Two Way
Continuous
Irreversible
Dynamic

Communication Is Continuous

We cannot not communicate. Even if we are not speaking, we are sending a message. We are always sending messages, and it seems the harder we try to not communicate, the louder our message becomes.

Every once in a while, I will get a few resistant participants in my communication seminars. It is obvious to me that these people want nothing to do with the program and that someone had encouraged them to be there against their will. Their closed body language tells me that they believe they have more important things to do with their time. Even though they may choose not to participate, they still communicate a message. That's why it's essential that we take an inventory of the messages we are sending.

Communication Is Irreversible

In the movie *When Harry Met Sally,* Billy Crystal, who plays Harry, says something to Sally played by Meg Ryan. Sally then says, "I can't believe you said that."

"Okay, I'll take it back," Harry says.

Sally then responds, "You can't take it back. Once you've said it, it's already out there."

Sally was right. When we communicate something, we send it out there, and we can't take it back. You can't unring the bell. Our *put in* is irreversible. If we want to receive maximum value in life, we need to be aware of what we are putting out into the world. People who are unaware of how the world perceives them are destined to repeat mistakes, encounter obstacles, and live a life of hardship.

One of my many jobs in my youth was as a bus loader  in Waikiki. It was my responsibility to ride the tour bus and find people who were looking for their tour and make sure that they made it on the bus. I had an employer who was a nice guy most of the time, but he seemed to be unaware as to how the world perceived him. If anyone made a mistake or didn't find the people who were supposed to be on the bus, he would go ballistic. He would scream on the radio, and when you came back to the office, he would once again let you know of your shortcomings. He ruled by fear, and his employees were

> *We are always communicating something and 100% of what you communicate is open to the interpretation of others. It goes out into the world, and you can't take it back.*

motivated not to do a good job but to stay out of trouble.

Every week during our meetings, he would ask for feedback for how to make our job better. I know that he was well meaning, and that he probably perceived himself as someone who was open to feedback and implementing change, but every week we would say that everything was fine.

It was always the most uncomfortable part of the week because everyone was thinking the same thing. "Well, we are all doing our best out there, and if you would just trust that we are doing everything we can, then stop yelling at us. Our workplace would improve considerably."

We have all worked in environments that are dominated by complacency and fear. As leaders, we must be aware of the messages we are sending and how they affect the people around us.

Communication Is Dynamic

In the movie *Groundhog Day,* Bill Murray plays a TV personality who is sent out to report on the groundhog day celebration in Pennsylvania. Every day, he wakes up again to relive the same groundhog day. As the movie progresses, we learn that even though everything else is the same, he is changing. Everyone is having the same experience, but he is learning, changing, and growing.

Communication happens the same way. If you were to have the exact same thing happen to you tomorrow as you did today, the experience would be different because you would have changed. That's why life is never boring. When we are bored, we choose to be bored.

Communication is always changing as well as the way we communicate. As we change, so do our strategies for communication. Mastering communication means learning to move past the barriers, which include:

Physical noise—Noise is defined as anything that blocks the communication process. Physical noise is the

most obvious type of noise. If you were trying to listen to instructions from someone and could not hear because the TV was blaring in the background, you have encountered physical noise.

Psychological noise—We all have voices in our heads running between 400 to 600 words per minute, every single moment of every day. Some of us have voices, and others of us have entire committees spouting off. These voices in our

heads are psychological noise, and they often become barriers to receiving information. Think about it. Have you ever been talking to someone and you knew he or she wasn't there? Has that ever been you? When have you pretended to pay attention to someone talking to you but you were thinking about what you were going to do this weekend? Have you ever been talking to someone while wondering what was hanging out of his or her nose? All of these are examples of psychological noise. Simply put: It is the voice inside of your head that keeps you from being present with the communication.

Physiological noise—If you have a hearing problem then you are challenged with physiological noise. This is an obvious barrier because you literally cannot hear the message. If you have a hearing problem, see a medical doctor to find out ways to remedy this situation.

Semantic noise—Have you ever been to a different part of the country and someone said something that you didn't understand? Chance are you were a victim of semantic noise. For example: How do you refer to your carbonated beverages? Where I am from, they are called pop. In some parts of the world, they are called soda. Others call them soda pop. If you go to the southern United States and order a coke, you will be asked what kind of coke you want: Pepsi, Mountain Dew, or Dr. Pepper.

In Wisconsin, I asked a principal where I could find the auditorium, and he told me to walk down the hallway and make a right at the bubbler. I had no idea that I was supposed to be looking for a water fountain.

Semantics is about word meaning, and it is the component of communication that makes communicating so dynamic. Every person hears a slightly different meaning when spoken to because we make sense of the world though a filter based upon our life experiences. If 100 people were in a room, and you gave one message, then 100 different messages would be received because everyone is receiving their message based upon their life experiences. It is a wonder that anything ever gets communicated clearly.

With so many barriers to communicating clearly, it becomes imperative that we have a strategy for understanding what messages we are putting out into the world so that we can communicate effectively. We must have an effective strategy for dealing with the many barriers to communication.

Strategy #1: Target Communication

We all have had teachers or professors who got off the subject and tended to wander aimlessly, talking about things

that had little to do with the subject. In fact, you may have even had strategies for getting the teacher off the subject so you wouldn't have to listen to the lecture but have a meaningless discussion instead. This can be fun in class, spending time with people who wander off the subject in business can be costly and time consuming.

Prior to any communication interaction, identify the target. Ask yourself: What do I hope to achieve as a result of this interaction? If you are walking into a meeting with a specific agenda of what you want to accomplish, that is a target. If you are having a

> *Ask yourself: What do I hope to achieve as a result of this interaction?*

phone conversation because you want a client to buy a product, then that is a target. If you want to get together with someone to develop your relationship, then you have identified your target. Target communication allows us to know whether or not we are achieving a result while interacting with others, and it gives us the ability to produce results.

Once you've identified your target, use your strategies for handling the barriers that may occur during your interaction. Your barriers might be psychological communication barriers: either yours or theirs. They might be semantic barriers. Your barriers might also be differing viewpoints, strategies for getting the job done, relational, or philosophical barriers. Using the earn-listening technique in strategy #2 helps us to communicate clearly, and to persuade with certainty so that both parties can walk away from an interaction feeling empowered and satisfied.

Strategy #2: Use the Earn-Listening Technique

Your first responsibility in any interaction is to listen to others so you can discover how their communication patterns represent their world. Use the earn-listening technique to figure this out. As you listen, ask yourself the following questions:

Essential: What is most important?

Action: Who benefits from this action?

Representation: How does this person represent this situation?

Needs: How will I communicate my needs?

Using *earn* is a discovery process that allows you to listen with clarity and communicate with conciseness.

Essential: What is most important to this person?—

Most of my communication with my clients begins with a phone conversation. Usually a client wants to get information about scheduling a date. I begin asking the *earn* questions. Not only am I listening to what is said, but how it is said and when it is said. If a client calls and asks right away about my fees, then I know that the most important factor in this conversation is probably price. It is on the top of this person's mind. Before I quote a price, however, I make discovery a priority.

Action: Who benefits from this action?—I want to know who this person sees as the key beneficiary from his or her request. I ask about specifics: about the audience, the organization's history with doing programs, the mission of the organization, and so on.

Representation: How do they represent this situation?—Even though this is a critical question, I would never ask it outright. It doesn't make any sense. You discover the answer to this question, however, by listening between the lines. I listen for key words, language patterns, tonality, and enthusiasm for the project. Since I already know in this situation that price is a main priority, I prepare myself for justifying the value of my program to this person.

Needs: How will I communicate my needs?—By listening closely to what is *essential*, who benefits from the *action*, and how this situation is *represented*, I can then articulate what I need. Remember: When you move into the other person's model of the world, you increase your chances of filling his or her needs.

Strategy #3: Look for Cues

As you listen, be on the lookout for clues that help you understand how a person represents the situation. There are two types of cues to listen for: tonality and contextual.

Tonality cues—Tonality cues have to do with the speed and tone at which the person is speaking. As you respond, match the person's speed so you move into that person's world. By doing so, you build rapport because subconsciously the person begins to think, "Hey, this person is just like me." If the person is a fast talker, listen to what makes him or her pause. If the person is a slow talker, listen to what

> *Tonality cues have to do with the speed and tone at which the person is speaking.*

causes him or her to speed up. Likewise, listen for things that cause a person to raise the pitch of his or her voice or lower it. All of these changes tell you what is important to the person. When you have gained rapport, then you will want to lead the person from time to time. By leading, I mean to change your inflection or speed and notice if the person changes as well. If the person comes along with you, then you can be assured that the two of you have rapport.

Contextual cues—Contextual cues tell you the context in which the person represents the situation. Contextual cues are either visual, auditory, or feeling. You can identify the context by listening to the person's language patterns. While listening discover which of the following patterns is the dominant context: visual, auditory or feeling.

Visual	Auditory	Feeling
I get the picture	That sounds good	It feels right
It is clear to me	I hear that	To get a handle,
Let's focus on	The key to this	I'm in touch with
My outlook is	I thought	Hard to handle
It shows up like	I was alarmed	This hits home

Now that you have really paid attention to this person, continue to ask about specifics that apply to your situation. Remember: Know your target so you can fill your needs as well as theirs. Even if I know from the get go that the person is concerned about price, I need to know how he or she represents the situation first. Otherwise I may not get my target, which is the speaking opportunity.

Strategy #4: Negotiate

Life is a series of negotiations, and we are always negotiating to fill our needs as well as the needs of others. By this point, you now have plenty of information and you are prepared to negotiate. Using the person's tonality and contextual cues, I quote my price by communicating in the same tonality, speed, pause patterns, and context.

If the person was highly auditory I would *say* something

like, "*Sounds* like it is important to you that your group is entertained and that people leave the program *talking* about what they learned so they can *teach* it to others...."

If the person was a visual communicator, I would say something that would stimulate their visual model of the world. An example of this would *show up* like this: "*Looks* like it is *pretty* important that people have a fun while *focusing* on getting a *clear* message...."

If the person was feeling oriented, I would communicate a message that would *get in touch* with their *senses*. A good example would be the following feeling statement: "This *feels* like a *fit* to me, and I know you want people to *move* forward and leave there *feeling* like they had fun, while learning some *hands-on* skills to *apply* in the future...."

State your needs. Then quit talking. So many times, people negotiate themselves out of what they want, and the other person never has to say a thing. I called a guy to give me an estimate on removing a diseased elm tree in my backyard. I told him what I wanted to have done and inquired about the cost. (The cost was important to me.) He told me he would do it for $1,000. I didn't say anything, so he kept talking.

"Well, I have a week open right now so, if I could start on Tuesday, I could do it for a little less. Then if you keep some of the wood as firewood so I don't have to haul it off, then I could do it for $750."

So I got a cord of wood and $250 off the price without

saying a word.

After you state your needs, wait for a response. Since you have been listening, you will know by the person's language patterns how close you are to filling his or her needs. Allow the person time to sort through the information. Ask questions that will move the person towards action.

For example, ask: "Would you like me to mail the contract or fax it?" "If we did this, when would you like the project to begin?"

After you begin the project, check in about further specifics. For example: "Since we're going to Disney World, which hotel would you like to stay in?"

Our Ability to Communicate

The quality of our communication determines the response we get. When we target our communication, we move past some of the barriers that naturally come with communication. Barriers such as psychological noise and semantic noise can easily be avoided when we really listen. Likewise we can eliminate differing viewpoints, strategies for getting the job done, relational, or philosophical barriers by using the *earn*-listening technique. This strategy will support you in finding the needs of others while accomplishing your goals.

Does this technique always work? That wouldn't be realistic, and it could be manipulative if it did. Our goal isn't to manipulate others into getting what we want. Instead our goal is to express our needs and discover if we can fill someone else's needs.

YOGOWYPI UNIVERSITY

*Define and discuss the communication process.

*Why is it important that we understand the communication process and how can this knowledge support us in avoiding potential communication challenges?

*Are you a good communicator? Why or why not? What are the qualities of a good communicator?

*Discuss the four barriers in the communication process. Of these four barriers which do you have the most control over? Which do you have the least control over?

*Have you ever had a boss, employer or parent who encouraged open, honest communication, but you were afraid to open up and be honest with them? Were your fears justified? Why or why not? What do they need to do differently to encourage a better stream of communication between the two of you?

*What are the qualities of a good listener? Do you know anyone who is very good at giving instructions, relaying messages, but are very poor listeners? Is this type of person common.? Discuss the connection between being a good listener and good communicator?

Do a role play using the EARN strategy. In this role play, have one person be a professor, and the other be a student who feels his or her grade was unjustified. Student role players, since you are the person in the interaction who has the desired gain be sure to listen to how they represent the situation and mirror those cues back to the professor. Professor role players, notice how you feel when the students works to move into your model of the world.

What is your dominant model of the world? Is it visual, auditory, or feeling oriented? Do you change your dominant interaction according to the situation? Over the next few days notice the communication patterns of those around you. Does learning to listen this way change your approach to others? What would happen if we constantly worked to understand others needs instead of always working to seek out our needs first?

Take a look at the following professions and identify what is the dominant interaction strategy of these occupations. Why do you think they would possibly have a dominant strategy?

    -Doctor
    -Lawyer
    -Architect
    -Counselor
    -Welder
    -Interior Decorator
    -Teacher/Professor
    -Sales Person
    -Emergency Medical Technician

The **YOGOWYPA** *Review*

People-People Understand Communication

Communication is a continuous, two way, irreversible, dynamic process.

The four types of noise in communication are physical, psychological, physiological and semantic.

Target communication is the process of asking yourself prior to the interaction what you hope to gain from this communication session.

The EARN Listening Technique. Essential, Action, Representation and Needs.

Look for cues. There are two types. Tonality and Contextual cues.

Tonality focuses on the tone at which people speak, as well as their rate. Listen for changes in tonality to understand what is important to the sender.

Contextual cues define how a person represents the situation. They are visual, auditory and feeling oriented.

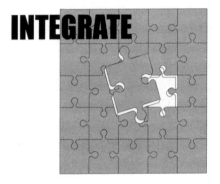

Chapter 12
I = Integration

Years ago, I was asked to do an all-school assembly in a Virginia community. I was to speak to 1:00 to 2:00 p.m., and then the students were scheduled for spring break at 2:15. This is a tough timeslot for any speaker, and even harder for the rookie that I was at the time.

I started my program, and the students were talking and moaning. One student in the back used some sign language to show that he thought I was number one. (He didn't use his index finger, but an alternative finger instead.) Other students started making inappropriate comments. I finally lost total control of the audience, and I stopped. "I don't feel respected right now," I said, "and I am leaving."

As I left, the students applauded. I proceeded down the hallway when the principal yelled, "Excuse me, Mr. Cordes, but you are not really going to leave, are you?"

"Yep," I said. "I am gone." On the inside, I was sure I had chosen the wrong profession. Only three months before that, I had left an excellent job with benefits to pursue this dream. Now I was walking out. I had decided I was going to get on that plane, go home, and start looking for a new job.

As I flipped through the million reasons to quit, the principal said, "You know, we have had a lot of speakers here before, and you are not doing that bad." Then he paused and asked, "Will you come back?"

The Voice

Just then, I heard the voice of Dr. Costigan. I remembered a lecture he gave during the last month of his life. He had been going through chemotherapy, and he was quite weak. He was talking about fear and how fear can be a great motivator to guide us and direct us. I remembered him saying, "Fear is a part of us, but it doesn't have to limit us. In fact, sometimes when we have fear, we should have the fear and do it anyway."

Sometimes when you're in a critical, defining moment, a voice appears. For me, it was Dr. Costigan. Even though he had been dead for a number of years, here was his voice, speaking to me loud and clear.

You will meet people with such a profound influence on you in your life that in moments of decision you will hear their voice. Just as Dr. Costigan was the voice for me, you get to be the voice for someone else. You get to live beyond yourself by living a life that matters. This is so much so that in times of decision, someone will look at your life and draw courage from your demonstration. I hope that as a result of applying the YOGOWYPI Factor in your life that you will be the voice for someone else, just as Dr. Costigan was the voice for me.

I looked at the principal and said, "I'll go back."

I went back, stood in front of the students, and I waited for them to get ready. Once it was relatively quiet, I started to talk. Those 20 remaining minutes with those students were my best 20 minutes of speaking up until that point in my career. If I had kept walking, I would have missed that opportunity. I would have felt like a total failure, and I probably would not be speaking today.

Breaking Through Instead of Breaking Down

It is the moments that we choose to apply what we know that become the essence of the YOGOWYPI Factor in our lives. It is those moments that we look inside of ourselves and make a decision that says, "Today I will stand up, and choose not what is comfortable for me but what is best for me and my future." It is making the choice to integrate all of what you know and then to accept the consequenses of your choice because you know that you are choosing according to principle and not according to the path of least resistance.

Integrating the **YOGOWYPI Factor** into our daily choices is really what we have been discussing all along. It is having the courage to first realize, **You Choose** your actions, your approach and your life situation. For me, I chose to be there in that moment doing that all-school assembly. I chose to walk out. I had a small window of opportunity to choose a different, better path.

It is knowing your **O-zone** and being aware that sometimes we choose out of conditioning and comfort. I walked out because I wanted out, but taking the time to understand the big picture gave me fuel for making a better choice. Better choices make our future better.

It is knowing that **Great Efforts Yield Great Rewards,**

and we can't expect the best if we don't do everything in our power to make our lives better. I have realized many times, just as I did in the moment that I decided to return to the assembly, that I can't make a difference if I choose to give up.

It is understanding the life-sustaining force of **O₂ Be**

Responsible. Just as oxygen gives us the ability to sustain life, it is responsibility that sustains our life choices. We can choose to feel bad, blame others, deny, or even quit. However, it is accepting where we are, learning from our mistakes, and then using them as an opportunity to grow that gives us real power in life.

Wisdom of Mission gives us energy, a sense of power and direction to press on when the times are tough, when we feel that we are alone and we need something to believe in. It is our compass that allows us to check for consistency in our life decisions. It is having the confidence of knowing that we are moving in the direction of our purpose and vision to push onward.

Y2Learn gives us the one element in our lives in which we can shape our future. Develop a burning desire to learn, grow and improve ourselves. Have the ability to tap into the resources of our brain to solve challenges and gain knowledge, and experiences that cannot be taken from us.

Knowing that we are ***People-People by Design*** gives us the power to know that we are never alone, and that if we tap into our network of people, we can communicate our challenges with clarity so that others can support us in our vision.

Then having the ability to ***Integrate*** all of these elements in an instant empowers us and those around us to live a life that makes an impact. It is learning to constantly assess where you are and what would be the best choice in each moment. Integration is the process of challenging yourself to develop new skills and positive patterns of behavior.

I learned several valuable lessons during that all-school assembly in Virginia. I learned that if people think they can push you to a certain point, then they will take you there just for the ride. However, when you are committed and persistent, then you create a different presence about yourself. This presence can withstand the power of others pushing you around.

I also learned that sometimes in life, we feel that we are in breakdown. Unfortunately, too many people think that breakdown is the end point, but it is not. On the other side of breakdown is breakthrough. When we learn to rely upon the wisdom of those who have gone before us, we can use their support and encouragement to get us though the challenging times so that we can make decision of which we are proud.

So now as you move forward into the life you've always wanted, remember: the wise words of Dr. Costigan: YOGOWYPI: You Only Get Out What You Put In. YOGOWYPI.

The **YOGOWYPI** *Review*

Integrate all of the individual components of
The YOGOWYPI Factor into your decision process
so you can make quality life choices.

Y = You Choose Your Approach

O = O-zone

G = Great Efforts Yield Great Rewards

**O = O$_2$ Oxygen: Responsibility
        Makes It Work**

W = Wisdom of Mission

Y = Y$_2$Learn

P = People Are "People-People" by Design

I = Integrate

Notes

[1] George Bernard Shaw, "Epistle Dedicatory to Aurthor Bingham Walkley," which appears before his play *Man and Superman,* which was originally published in 1903. George Bernard Shaw, *Plays by George Bernard Shaw,* (Mattituck, New York: Amereon House), 257

[2] George Bernard Shaw, *Essex Daily News* (Brighton, England), March 7, 1907.

[3] George Bernard Shaw, 1856-1950, wrote more than 50 plays in his lifetime. He was awarded the Nobel Prize in Literature in 1925. He accepted the honor but refused the accompanying prize money. He died at the age of 94 while at work on another play.

About the Author

Bill D. Cordes is a speaker, consultant and author. He has keynoted programs for conferences, conventions, schools and universities nationwide. His programs have been featured in 44 states. Bill has co-authored numerous books for teens including, *Teen Power Too, Teen Empower, Teen Power Through Christ, Lead Now or Step Aside, and Teen Power and Beyond.*

Bill did his graduate and undergraduate work at the University of Hawaii and Fort Hays State University. He was awarded Graduate Student Teacher of the Year by the International Communication Association while teaching at Fort Hays State University. Bill is a committed Christian, husband and father of three wonderful children. In his programs, Bill combines humor, enthusiasm and draws on his extensive life experience of being a former teacher, college instructor, coach and television talk show host.

Contact Bill through Cordes Keynotes and Seminars, 5327 Quail Creek, Great Bend, Kansas 67530. 1-800-401-6670; www.billcordes.com or email at yogowypi@aol.com.